30 Days with Elijah

Pointers from Elijah's
Spiritual Journey for Yours

(A Devotional)

STEVE WILMOT

Copyright © 2022 Steve Wilmot
All rights reserved.

No part of this book may be reproduced, or stored in a retrieval system, or transmitted in any form or by any means, electronic, mechanical, photocopying, recording, or otherwise, without express written permission of the publisher.

All Scripture quotations, unless otherwise indicated, are taken from the Holy Bible, New International Version®, NIV®. Copyright ©1973, 1978, 1984, 2011 by Biblica, Inc.™ Used by permission of Zondervan. All rights reserved worldwide. www.zondervan.com The "NIV" and "New International Version" are trademarks registered in the United States Patent and Trademark Office by Biblica, Inc.™

Scripture quotations marked (NLT) are taken from the Holy Bible, New Living Translation, copyright ©1996, 2004, 2015 by Tyndale House Foundation. Used by permission of Tyndale House Publishers, Carol Stream, Illinois 60188. All rights reserved.

Paperback ISBN — 978-1-7348043-7-9

Cover design by: xheheryaar

Printed in the United States of America

First Edition

Dedication

This devotional is dedicated to a wonderful group of new friends at Harvest Fellowship in Ft. Wayne, Indiana.

They participated in a Sunday school class I taught on Elijah and contributed some of the insights included in this devotional.

Members of the class include:
Gary & Diane Allen
Scott & Tieriyn Benjamin
Kim Bowker
Eric & Lindsey Braun
Bob Herman
Randy Hunt
Steve & Barb Jennings
Tim Labie
Whit & Jen Longcore
David & Julia Overy
Betsy Weiss
Ken & Patricia Weiss
Tom & Marcy Zeissig

Thank you, Whit, for co-teaching this class with me and for your dedication to the Word of God.

TABLE OF CONTENTS

Introduction 9

1. Conformed to Culture.................................... 13
2. From Out of Nowhere 19
3. Elijah's Gravestone... 25
4. The War Begins 29
5. "There" 33
6. A Change in Plan 37
7. The Greatest Fact 41
8. The Blame Game 47
9. Into the Unknown 51
10. Obedience is a Big Deal to God 55
11. A Godly Man in an Ungodly Culture 59
12. Gotta Choose 65
13. Prove It 71
14. Nothing is too Hard for God........................ 75
15. Relentless.. 79

16.	Let It Rain	85
17.	Roots of Depression	89
18.	A Way Out of Depression	95
19.	Perspective	101
20.	A Task and a Friend	105
21.	A Whisper	111
22.	The Cost of the Call	117
23.	The Final Straw	123
24.	Merciful God	129
25.	Your Verse	135
26.	Practical Atheists	141
27.	Escape Clause	145
28.	What Can I Do For You?	149
29.	Homecoming	155
30.	Elijahs of God	161
About Steve		167
Other Books by Steve		167
Connect with Steve!		182

INTRODUCTION

30 Days with Elijah: Pointers from Elijah's Spiritual Journey for Yours is the third in a series of devotionals written to pick up pointers from Bible characters for our spiritual journey. Elijah's story is uniquely helpful because *"Elijah was a man just like us"* (James 5.17). To trace his life is to look in a mirror at our own.

Elijah was as human as we are. He's not so other-than-us it makes us believe it's impossible for us to match his faith, his prayer life, or his walk with God. He battled the same roller coaster of emotions we do. He experienced life from both ends of the spectrum like we do — from periods of undaunting courage and unwavering faith, to struggles with deep depression and frantic fear.

The story of Elijah shows us God can transform an average Christian into a person he can use despite our foibles and weaknesses.

Elijah challenged a powerful king without wavering even with his life was on the line.

He devoted the best years of his life to prove Jehovah God was the only true God, and to call Israel to turn to the Lord God Almighty from the impotent, false gods they worshiped.

Elijah persevered even though he thought he was the only one loyal to God in the entire nation, and everyone was against him.

He endured the hardships of living as a Godly man in an ungodly culture — a culture not just indifferent to God but anti-God, making every effort to erase hum completely from their history, government, schools, and homes.

Above all, Elijah was a man who prayed and obeyed.

Because Elijah was no different than you and faced the same issues you do, and because God is the same God who works today the way he did in the days of Elijah, his story can become your story.

Wouldn't that make your life rewarding and exciting?

At the end of each day's reading, I've included an idea designed to help you pray or think about something that jumped out at you when you read the daily Scripture or the devotional. You'll find it under the heading "Run with it." I took the idea from instructions God gave Habakkuk: *"The Lord replied, 'Write down the revelation and make it plain on tablets so that whoever reads it may run with it'"* (Habakkuk 2.2).

God wants everyone who reads His Word to "*run with it,*" and not forget it the moment they close their Bible and check "Read Bible" off their to-do list. Your mind, your faith, your grasp on truth, and your actions should be influenced from what you read each day as you run with it.

While you can read these devotions anytime during the day, the best time is in the morning. It will give you the rest of the day to mull over the Word of God as you go about your daily activities. You offer God your whole day to speak to you, renew your mind, and transform your life.

DAY 1
Conformed to Culture

Ahab also made an Asherah pole and did more to provoke the Lord, the God of Israel to anger than did all the kings of Israel before him.
(1 Kings 16.33)

Read 1 Kings 16.29-34

In 1983, Aleksandr Solzhenitsyn received the Templeton Prize for Progress in Religion. Solzhenitsyn, an author who died in 2008 at the age of 89, is still one of the most famous critics of communism and its attack on Christianity.

In his acceptance speech, Solzhenitsyn recalled the words his elders taught him as a child to explain the continuous mayhem that rocked Russia. "Men have forgotten God; that's why all this has happened." He added, "If I were called upon to identify briefly the principal trait of the entire twentieth century, here too I would be unable to find anything more precise and pithy than to repeat once again: 'men have forgotten God.'"

Israel in the days of the prophet Elijah provides a prime example.

When Israel divided into the Northern Kingdom (Israel) and the Southern Kingdom (Judah), Israel's culture took a nosedive. Beginning with Jeroboam, every king of Israel encouraged the citizens of their kingdom to forget God and worship false gods.

Sixty-two years of political and spiritual decline passed before Ahab ascended the throne and took Israel's culture deeper into wickedness than ever. Over those six-plus decades, Israel transitioned from worshipers of God to a religion that mixed God with false gods. But Ahab took it further — he tried to completely eliminate God from Israel.

Ahab accelerated the downward spiral of an anti-god culture when he thumbed his nose at one of God's warnings — *"You must not intermarry with them* [the idol-worshiping nations surrounding them], *because they will surely turn your hearts after their gods"* (1 Kings 11.2; see also Deuteronomy 7.3-6).

Ahab ignored God's command and married Jezebel, daughter of the king of the Sidonians. She easily persuaded her lukewarm husband to worship Baal. One hundred percent sold out to Baal, Jezebel embarked on a campaign to assassinate every prophet of God and silence their voices.

With Jezebel as a catalyst, *"Ahab... did more to provoke the Lord, the God of Israel, to anger than did all the kings of Israel before him"* (1 Kings 16.33). Here's a

partial list of what Ahab did to earn this assessment from God:
- He replaced God with Baal as the deity to serve. Baal worship included animal and child sacrifices, sexual rituals, and occultism.
- He built a temple and set up an altar to Baal in the capitol city of Samaria. It provided a subtle way to cut Israel's centuries-old devotion to God and substitute Baal in his place.
- He joined Jezebel when she instigated a crusade to kill every one of the Lord's prophets to remove God from the nation's conscience.

To suggest Ahab and Jezebel had no influence on Israel's culture is folly. The culture they created forced the prophets who escaped Jezebel's holocaust into hiding and nominal believers into silence. The couple stifled anything related to the worship of God and promoted everything they could to turn the nation to false gods.

This is the culture God sent Elijah to confront. It wasn't easy, but as you'll read in the next chapters, Elijah met the challenge because he knew God was with him.

Like Elijah, we live in a culture trying to eliminate God from it. We can see daily Solzhenitsyn was right when he claimed forgetting God was the pivotal negative influence on a culture. How do you respond to the anti-god culture we live in today?

Sadly, many Christians conform — blending in and remaining quiet. In his book *Your Jesus Is Too Safe*, Jared Wilson notes that "in American culture, it has often become hard to distinguish between the body of Christ and the culture of society."

Surveys show little disparity in the moral standards and lifestyle of Christians and non-Christians. The divorce rate is 50 percent for both Christian and non-Christian marriages. Seventy-six percent of Christian singles don't consider pre-marital sex a sin. Sixty-five percent of all abortions are performed on women who profess a Christian faith.

Researcher George Barna reports less than 10 percent of born-again Christians have a "biblical worldview," i.e., a core set of convictions and beliefs they hold as absolute truth.

Rather than conform to this ungodly culture, we Christians must anchor ourselves against the current and live as serious followers of Jesus Christ.

Daniel lived in a pagan culture that did everything it could to force him to conform. *"But Daniel resolved not to defile himself"* (Daniel 1.8). He vowed he would not conform... and he didn't. How did he do it?

For one, Daniel partnered with three other guys who also determined they would not get sucked into the wicked culture of the Babylonians (Daniel 1.7). You can't resist the tide of an anti-God culture alone. You must find strength by connecting with others who have made the same decision.

Daniel also continued to live for God the way he always had. When the king outlawed prayer, Daniel maintained his three-times-a-day prayer habit even though he knew punishment awaited if caught. He loved and worshiped God *"just as he had done before"* (Daniel 6.10-11).

Elijah stepped into an anti-God culture that was going downhill with ever increasing velocity. He came to prove to Israel the God they once worshiped, not Baal, was the one true God, and to let them know God was turning their hearts back to him again.

Run with it:
Ponder how you will resist conformity to our culture and what you can do to influence it.

DAY 2

From Out of Nowhere

Now Elijah the Tishbite, from Tishbe in Gilead, said to Ahab...
(1 Kings 17.1a)

Read 1 Kings 17.1

The Lone Ranger was a superhero before superheroes were popular. First appearing as a radio program, his trademark was a silver bullet and a mask he never removed in public. When trouble arose in a Western town, there he was with his faithful companion, Tonto. He just popped in from out of nowhere, rescued the damsel in distress, and rode off to the next town.

A television program followed his exploits in the early 50s. Each episode (221 in all over five seasons) ended with the same scene. The Lone Ranger hopped aboard his horse and spurred him on to their next destination with a hearty, "Hi-ho, Silver! Away!"

As he rode off into the distance, someone in the town would always look at the person next to him and ask, "Who was that masked man?" No one ever knew.

Like the Lone Ranger, Elijah showed up one day from out of nowhere. He came to save King Ahab and the nation from the judgment of God. His message to Ahab informed him that God would withhold rain and dew for several years until Elijah prayed and God sent rain.

Unlike those the Lone Ranger came to rescue, Ahab wasn't excited to see Elijah. After all, the first words out of the prophet's mouth declared the Lord was the God of Israel, not the false gods Ahab pedaled to God's chosen people. Ahab wanted nothing to do with God — he was determined to erase God from the Israeli culture and replace him with a false god, Baal.

Ahab and his foreign wife Jezebel had already made inroads toward that end. They had destroyed the altars of God and built a temple to Baal, complete with an altar to offer him sacrifices. They had killed many of God's prophets, and God wasn't mentioned anymore, let alone worshiped.

At this crucial time in the history of Israel, Elijah suddenly appeared as God's man with an urgent message. Ordinarily, when God raised up a new prophet as his mouthpiece, the Bible writer provides some personal background — who his father is, what tribe he belongs to, etc. But not with Elijah. One minute, no one knows he exists. The next, he's confronting a powerful, anti-God king.

Elijah became the dominant spiritual force in Israel during the dark days of Ahab's apostasy. And though his impact on Israel is told in a mere six chapters, he became one of God's most important prophets.

Matthew Henry describes Elijah in glowing terms. "One might have expected God would cast off a people that had so cast him off; but, as evidence to the contrary, never was Israel so blessed with a good prophet as when it was so plagued with a bad king. Never was a king so bold to sin as Ahab; never was a prophet so bold to reprove and threaten as Elijah."

Where are the Elijahs of God in our anti-God culture?

Just as Elijah showed up from out of nowhere to Ahab with a word from God, you will unexpectedly cross paths with someone God puts in your way. Someone he wants you to pray for or befriend or offer a word of encouragement to or lead to a saving relationship with Jesus.

Sometimes it'll be an unintended encounter — God just puts you in the same space as the person he wants you to help. This person may be an acquaintance or a total stranger, but God arranged the connection so you can be the conduit through whom God speaks.

Other times, God will prompt you to visit someone who needs encouraged or comforted or challenged. Sometimes they'll be in a tough situation that overwhelms them and God wants you there to make sure they don't go through it alone. Many times he'll want you to embolden their faith by reminding them of his promises and all of the times he showed up for them in the past.

The thing is, God often works behind the scenes to advance a person's God-designed destiny, and he uses you as a part of his plan.

From out of nowhere, Elijah answered God's call even though it was risky and inconvenient. He had lived a quiet life in obscurity with family and friends, but now he stands on the front lines in a spiritual war for Israel's soul.

From out of nowhere, Ananias answered God's call to restore Saul/Paul's blindness that resulted from his encounter with Jesus on the road to Damascus. He went even though he knew it could cause his death. [Acts 9.1-19]

From out of nowhere, Barnabas took Saul/Paul under his wing and vouched for him when the church worried he was undercover and not a genuine disciple of Jesus. [Acts 9.26-28]

You can be an Ananias or a Barnabas to a Saul/Paul. An Elijah to an Ahab. God wants to hook you up with those he wants to touch. He may arrange things so you cross paths with them, or he may tap you on the shoulder and urge you to go see them. Either way, you will show up in their moment of need from out of nowhere as God's representative… if you'll let him.

Run with it:

Thank God for a time he sent someone to you from out of nowhere in your hour of need. Why not pay it forward and tell God you're willing to be an Elijah whenever he needs you.

DAY 3

Elijah's Gravestone

"So he did what the Lord told him."
(1 Kings 17.5)

Read 1 Kings 17.1-5

Inscriptions on gravestones give a snapshot of a dead person's life. Some warm the heart; others break it.

A son about his father: "Always gone; still is."

"Uncle Walter loved to spend. He had no money in the end. But with many a whiskey and many a wife, he really did enjoy his life."

"To our mother: You spent your life expressing animosity for nearly every person you encountered, including your children. Within hours of his death, you even managed to declare your husband of 57 years unsuited to be either a spouse or a father. Hopefully, you are now insulated from all the dissatisfaction you found in human relationships."

If someone condensed Elijah's life into a tombstone-size recap, it would read something along this line: "He prayed and he obeyed."

These two words describe Elijah's life to a T, and they are the primary reasons God worked in the extraordinary ways he did in him and through him.

He prayed.

As you read the story of Elijah, you'll see God do many miraculous things because he prayed. In six brief Bible chapters which record his life, you can find at least four miracles result as an answer to his prayers.

1. He prayed to stop the rain, and it didn't rain for three-and-one-half years (1 Kings 17.1).
2. He asked God to bring the widow's son back to life, and God did (I Kings 17.19-22).
3. He prayed for fire from heaven on Mt. Carmel to burn up his sacrifice, and God sent it almost before Elijah finished praying (1 Kings 18.36-39).
4. He prayed for God to send rain and end the drought, and the heavens opened and poured down rain (1 Kings 18.41-45).

When we read such dramatic answers to prayer, it's easy to wish we could pray and have the same effect Elijah did. We can!

That's one problem most Christians run into when they look at their prayer life and compare it to the prayer lives of the heroes of the faith. We jump to the conclusion God won't answer our prayers the way he did Elijah's because he was special, someone a cut above us. But that's a lie from Satan to discourage us from asking God to do extraordinary feats in our lives and in the lives of those we pray for.

"Elijah was a man just like us. He prayed earnestly it would not rain, and it did not... Again he prayed, and the heavens gave rain" (James 5.17-18). Did you catch that? Elijah experienced the same <u>struggles, problems, emotional roller coasters, and fears you</u> do. So pray and watch God answer in amazing ways. *"The prayer of* [any] *righteous man* [Christian] *is powerful and effective"* (Jas. 5.16).

"Prayer turns ordinary mortals into people of power. It brings power. It brings fire. It brings rain. It brings life. It brings God" (Samuel Chadwick).

He obeyed.

From the opening verses of Elijah's story, we find a consistent pattern of obedience to God.

1. God told Elijah to go to the Kerith Ravine... *"So he did what the Lord told him"* (1 Kings 17.2-5).
2. God told him to go to Zarephath... *"So he went"* (1 Kings 17.9-10).
3. God sent him to Ahab... *"So Elijah went to present himself to Ahab"* (1 Kings 18.1-2).
4. God told him to anoint three men he had chosen for important assignments... *"So Elijah went"* (1 Kings 19.15-19).
5. God sent him to confront Ahab concerning his sin against Naboth and pronounce his punishment... and Elijah obeyed (1 Kings 21.17-22).

6. God sent him to ask the messengers of King Ahaziah regarding a faith issue... *"So Elijah went"* (2 Kings 1.3-4).
7. God told him to meet Ahaziah face-to-face... *"So Elijah got up and went"* (2 Kings 1.15).

Obedience is one of the common denominators in each and every great man and woman of God. Noah (Genesis 6.22; 7.50); Abraham (Genesis 12.1-4; 22.2-3); Peter (Luke 5.4-5); Ananias (Acts 9.10-18); Mary (Luke 2.1.30-38); the widow of Zarephath (1 Kings 17.13-15); every hero of the faith catalogued in Hebrews 11.

Can anything please God more than watching his children obey him, even when it's terrifying and risky? Even when it makes no sense to us?

Since Elijah was exactly like us and God is forever unchanging, he will do the same in you and through you that he did with Elijah... if "he/she prayed and obeyed" becomes the distinguishing characteristic of your life.

Run with it:

Contemplate what your tombstone will read to summarize your life. Ask God to show you. If you're not happy with this abridged biography, what will you do to change it while you can?

DAY 4
The War Begins

"Now Elijah... said to Ahab, 'As the Lord, the God of Israel, lives, whom I serve, there will be neither dew nor rain in the next few years except at my word.'"
(1 Kings 17.1)

Years ago, the Exxon Valdez oil spill in Alaska sparked an environmental crisis. The massive rescue effort included cleaning-up oil-soaked seals at the average cost of $80,000 per seal. Environmentalists held a special ceremony for the release of two of the saved seals back into the wild. Loud cheers and applause from the crowd celebrated their recovery as they swam away.

A minute later, a killer whale ate both seals.

Now that's a bad day. Sort of like the day King Ahab met Elijah for the first time. Elijah relayed a message from God that rocked him and his nation's world. God, Elijah announced, had decided to withhold rain from the land.

This marked the first salvo in a war between God and Baal to show who was the true God. Since the death of Joshua, Israel gradually replaced the Lord God as their object of worship with the pagan god Baal. They believed

Baal was the sky god who controlled the weather. Elijah appeared to challenge their assumption and prove the God he represented, not Baal, decided when it would rain and when it wouldn't.

Thus, we have a contest to investigate the claims of these two competing deities. There can only be one God who rules supreme and all others are fakes. Elijah intended to prove to Ahab and the Israelites the God who led them out of Egypt with a mighty hand was the one true God.

It's a simple test with indisputable evidence to reveal who the true God is. If the God of Elijah restrained the rain, then [a] he is God, [b] Israel should abandon Baal and return to God, [c] Elijah is his spokesman, and [d] the Israelites had better listen to what Elijah says.

But if Baal overrode God's decree and sent rain, then [a] he is god, [b] Israel should continue to follow him and renounce this nonsense Elijah is pushing, [c] Baal's prophets are his spokesmen, and [d] the Israelites had better listen to what they say.

Spoiler alert: God prevented rain for three years, plus later did other feats to prove he was God. Yet the war for the heart of the nation was lost because they chose the impotent impostor, Baal.

We fight this war against the heart for control of the heart in every generation. It's the prize God and your enemy Satan wants to conquer because whoever rules it controls the person: *"everything you do flows from it"* (Proverbs 4.23). Your thoughts, emotions, words, actions, attitudes, priorities, worldview, values, and responses to situations and people flow from your heart.

You were born into a world at war, though maybe you haven't discovered it yet. That's Satan's greatest advantage. When you're unaware there's a war going on and you are the target, you don't fight back. This war isn't fought with bullets and bombs; its weapons are thoughts and emotions. The outcome of each battle is determined by the choice you make about where to turn with those thoughts and emotions.

The gods of the twenty-first century don't come shaped as cast metal idols. Kyle Idleman, in his book *Gods at War,* asks, "What if [the gods of here and now] take identities so ordinary that we don't recognize them as gods at all? What if we do our 'kneeling' and our 'bowing' with our imaginations, our checkbooks, our search engines, our calendars?"

The gods of today go by different names — pleasure, wealth, success, sex, approval, escape, fame, power, people, possessions, popularity, etc. — but they are as seductive as Baal ever was. They promise help but only deliver disappointment, chains, and dependency.

Here are a few examples of how the war is fought:

The enemy stirs up anxiety in you. Do you run to God in prayer to receive peace beyond understanding (Philippians 4.6-7), or do you run to the refrigerator for a plate of "comfort food"? That decision — God or some other god, in this case food — determines whether God or Satan wins the battle for first place in your heart.

The enemy wears you down with weariness from dealing with a difficulty that's lingered for a long time or a strained relationship. Do you turn to God who gives strength to the weary and increases the power of the weak (Isaiah 40.19) as your first resort, or do you turn to the god alcohol to numb the pain for a while?

The enemy attacks with depression. Do you fix your hope in God that things won't stay like this forever (Psalm 42.5), or do you surrender to the temptation for a temporary high from pornography?

There is an endless supply of gods you can pick from as substitutes for the Lord God. The choice is up to you. If you opt for a lesser god, you'll be disappointed every time. They may give short-term relief, but it never lasts, so you're left to hope it works next time. Or give a different god a try expecting it to do what the others you've tried before haven't.

Concerning your options, Jeremiah, the prophet, observed, *"Nor can* [idols] *do any good. No one is like you, O Lord; you are great, and your name is mighty in power"* (Jeremiah 10.5b-6). Seems like the choice is easy.

Run with it:

Shortly before his death, Joshua left Israel with a momentous choice that would affect every aspect of their lives from then on. *"Choose this day whom you will serve"* (Joshua 24.15). You must choose daily. Who do you choose today?

DAY 5
"There"

"You will drink from the brook, and I have ordered the ravens to feed you there."
(1 Kings 17.4)

Read 1 Kings 17.2-6

Do you ever wonder why…
- Women can't put on mascara with their mouth closed
- They make lemon juice with artificial flavor and dishwashing liquid with real lemons
- The man who invests your money is called a broker
- There isn't mouse-flavored cat food
- Noah didn't swat those two mosquitoes
- Sheep don't shrink when it rains

Probably not. They're conundrums most people never even notice, let alone wonder about. But how about this one: Do you ever wonder why God sometimes doesn't make good on his promises to you?

The answer is simple. Every promise has a premise — something God requires you to do before he fulfills his promise. Rick Warren says, "There are more than

5,000 promises in the Bible, and every one of them has a premise. *Every promise has a premise."*

Check out these three examples.

"Let us not become weary in doing good, for at the proper time we will reap a harvest if we do not give up" (Galatians 6.9). Promise: reap a harvest. Premise: don't give up.

"Do not be anxious about anything, but in everything, by prayer and petition, with thanksgiving, present your requests to God. And the peace of God... will guard your hearts and your minds in Christ Jesus" (Philippians 4.6-7). Promise: the peace of God in every stressful situation you find yourself. Premise: don't worry, pray instead.

"Honor the Lord with your wealth, with the firstfruits of all your crops. Then your barns will be filled to overflowing and your vats will brim over with new wine" (Proverbs 3.9-10). Promise: abundant supply. Premise: give God the first portion of your income.

You fulfill the premise; God follows through on his promise. Fail to fulfill the premise; God doesn't keep his promise.

God gives Elijah a promise moments after his first meeting with King Ahab. Elijah informed him God had decided to withhold rain to prove to him and the nation he was the only God in the universe. Didn't make Ahab happy. The approaching drought was a threat to his reign and to the northern kingdom of Israel he ruled.

Thus, Elijah's life was in danger. So God told him to hide in the Kerith Ravine and promised to provide food and water for him while the famine stripped the land of everything to eat and drink.

Promise: God will supply him with food and water throughout the drought. *"You will drink from the brook, and I have ordered ravens to feed you"* (verse 4).

Premise: go to the Kerith Ravine and stay *"there"* (verse 4). There. At the brook in the Kerith Ravine. Not at a place of Elijah's choosing. Not in a location where Elijah knew there was an ample supply of food for years to come. No. If Elijah wanted God to keep his word, Elijah had to go where God told him to go.

And, true to form, *"So he did what the Lord had told him. He went to the Kerith Ravine... and stayed there"* (verse 5). Elijah did what God told him to do (premise), and God kept his promise. Morning and evening, he sent ravens with bread and meat for Elijah, and the brook supplied him with an abundance of water.

When you find yourself in a situation where you need to claim a promise from God, always look for an attached premise. Some step of obedience or act of faith God expects from you as a condition for fulfilling his promise.

God always has a reason for demanding action on your part. You may not understand the purpose, but you don't have to. All you need to know is God intends to further his good plan for you and to advance his kingdom, and that demands a step of obedience on your part first.

For Elijah, the obvious benefit was his safety and provision through the famine. But there was a more important reason — to build his faith for what was ahead.

"I think there is another purpose for this three-and-one-half year period of hiding. This appears to be the commencement of Elijah's public ministry. It is important for this prophet to be deeply convinced of God's ability to provide for his every need, both for his daily provisions and for his protection. God is using this quiet time in Elijah's life to teach him to 'trust and obey'" (Anon).

Just like with Elijah, hidden in the premise of God's promise to you is a benefit with far greater value than the promise alone. You'll learn to depend on God. Your faith will be strengthened — "If God was faithful then, I can count on him to be faithful now." God will prepare you for what's ahead in your life — the challenges and the victories. You'll develop endurance, a consistent prayer life, and a greater appreciation for the genius of God.

Run with it:
In every promise, there is a premise. Find it and obey it. It will position you to enjoy great blessings and to see God work great wonders in you and through you.

DAY 6
A Change in Plan

Some time later, the brook dried up because there had been no rain in the land.
(1 Kings 17.7)

Read 1 Kings 17.7-9

When railroads were first introduced in the United States, some Americans feared they would ruin the nation. Here's an excerpt of a letter from Martin Van Buren, then governor of New York, to President Andrew Jackson in 1829.

"As you may know, Mr. President, railroad carriages are pulled at the enormous speed of 15 miles per hour by engines which, in addition to endangering life and limb of passengers, roar and snort their way through the countryside, setting fire to crops, scaring the livestock and frightening women and children. The Almighty certainly never intended that people should travel at such breakneck speed."

Somebody doesn't like change. Governor Van Buren is in good company. Seems everyone hates and resists change. The Duke of Cambridge complained, "Any change, at any time, for any reason, is to be deplored." Mark Twain remarked, "The only person who likes change is a wet baby."

While unpopular and often resisted, "change is the only constant" in life, observed Greek philosopher Heraclitus of Ephesus. Change happens and it's unavoidable.

Elijah was on the brink of yet another change in his life. First, God called him out of comfortable obscurity to take an unsolicited message to King Ahab. Afterwards, God told him to flee to the Kerith Ravine and hide from Ahab. Now, after a year in which God met all of Elijah's physical needs, he changes the plan again. With the brook dried up from the lack of rain, God directs Elijah to Zarephath.

For Elijah to assume he'd stay at the brook for the duration of the drought seemed logical, but God had other plans. His plans don't always go the way we think they will. In fact, they rarely do. Have you discovered that yet?

God doesn't do things the way we would. His plans involve changes we never see coming. Though surprising and unexpected, changes in his plans are always good. In fact, these changes lead to better outcomes than we could ever imagine.

In God's game plan, change is more the rule than the exception.

Moses killed an Egyptian, supposing the enslaved Israelites would realize God was using him to rescue them. God wasn't and they didn't (see Acts 7.23-25). God changed Moses' location and sent him into the wilderness for 40 years to mold his character and perspective until it was time for God to send him back to Egypt to free his people.

God showed Joseph in a dream he would become an influential leader. But the path God led him on was unexpected, a path marked by jealousy, betrayal, slavery, and prison under false charges. Far different from the direction Joseph had imagined his life would take.

Mary and Joseph planned to get married, have a family, and live happily ever after, but God dramatically changed that.

On his way to Damascus with orders to arrest any Christians he found, Saul met Jesus and the whole direction and purpose of his life changed.

Same with Peter. He imagined an enjoyable life with his family and a career as a fisherman until he died, but God had other plans.

Don't be surprised if God changes your carefully laid plans for the future.

God had a special agenda for Elijah that required a change of scenery. Elijah needed another building block to strengthen his faith for the greater challenges to come. And there was a Gentile woman God wanted brought to faith who Elijah couldn't reach from the Kerith Ravine.

It's the same for you. God executes changes in your life and works behind the scenes to carry out his will for your life.

We see nothing from Elijah but trust in God as he transitions from the safety of the brook to Zarephath, a town in enemy territory, a mere eight miles from where Jezebel grew up. He doesn't complain. There's no worry, no fear, no questions, no demands of God for an explanation. Only trust and obedience.

Elijah understood, *"... my thoughts are not your thoughts, neither are your ways my ways, declares the Lord. For as the heavens are higher than the earth, so are my ways higher than your ways and my thoughts than your thoughts"* (Isaiah 55.9-10).

Good thing because *"There is a way that seems right to a man, but in the end it leads to death"* (Proverbs 14.12). To add emphasis and make sure we don't miss it, Solomon wrote it again in Proverbs 16.25.

God knows what he's doing, and he always fits the puzzle pieces of his plan together perfectly and in the right order. If left to us, we'd mess it up every time. But God is never wrong. He's never made a mistake, and he won't start with you.

When it comes to change, go with God.

Run with it:

Take a moment to evaluate how you react to change. Has your willingness to embrace change shifted after reading this devotional? How?

DAY 7

The Greatest Fact

For this is what the Lord, the God of Israel, says: "The jar of flour will not be used up and the jug of oil will not run out until the day the Lord gives rain on the land."
(1 Kings 17.14)

Read 1 Kings 17.7-16

"You can live on bland food so as to avoid an ulcer; drink no tea or coffee or other stimulants, in the name of health; go to bed early and stay away from night life; avoid all controversial subjects so as never to give offense; mind your own business and avoid involvement in other people's problems; spend money only on necessities and save all you can. You can still break your neck in the bathtub, and it will serve you right" (Eileen Guder, *God, But I'm Bored*).

The moral is: Don't play it safe; take some risks. Elijah challenged the widow of Zarephath when he asked her for a piece of bread. It didn't sound like a big deal, but for the widow and her son, it was huge. A year earlier, God stopped the rain from falling in Israel. Food was scarce, and for this poor widow, starvation looked inevitable.

She told Elijah she couldn't bring him anything to eat and spelled out three reasons:
1. She only had a handful of flour and a little oil in a jug.
2. She was on her way home to make a last meal for her son and herself.
3. Then they would die.

As Adam Clarke observes, "This was certainly putting the widow's faith to an extraordinary trial: to take and give to a stranger, of whom she knew nothing, the small pittance requisite to keep her child from perishing, was too much to be expected."

There was no candy coating her dire situation. Those were the facts as she saw things. But she either missed or ignored a greater fact Elijah told her when he asked her for bread. God, Elijah said, will keep her jar of flour and jug of oil full until he sent rain and ended the famine if she made Elijah a small cake of bread first.

Just like we often do, the widow based her decision on a set of facts that seemed logical: We've only enough food for one meal before we die. I can't feed you. But also like us, she overlooked the most important fact of all — God never fails to do what he says he will do if we step out in faith.

But first, she must take the risk. One that could potentially deprive them of their last meal.

This widow was not a woman of faith; she was a Gentile who identified God as Elijah's God, not hers. This was an enormous gamble for her.

We don't have insight into her decision-making process, but it's easy to imagine it went something like this: "If I use all the flour and oil and make a final meal for my son and me, we'll run out of food and we *will* die for sure. If I make a meal for Elijah first, we *might* die ... or maybe not. Perhaps his God will do what Elijah says he'll do. Oh shoot, I'll make the meal for Elijah and see what happens."

We know how the story ends. The widow made Elijah a meal from the rest of her supplies and God kept his promise. *"So there was food every day for Elijah and for the woman and her family. For the jar of flour was not used up and the jug of oil did not run dry, in keeping with the word of the Lord spoken by Elijah"* (1 Kings 17.15-16).

The fulfillment of God's promise is stated so matter-of-factly. As if it wasn't a big deal. No surprise here. God said he'd do something if you did something first; you did and so he did. Simple and totally expected.

Whenever you factor God into an equation, you can throw the facts and conclusions that seem logical out the window. There are facts… and there are greater facts — the promises of God, the faithfulness of God, the goodness of God, the generosity of God, and the power of God to keep every promise he's ever made. His track record of promises kept is flawless.

That's the advantage you have over the widow. She didn't have a history with God; no personal experience of his faithfulness; no "if he did it then, he'll do it again now." But you do. You're confident you can trust God. You have proof. You've read documentation in the Bible. Here's just one example out of thousands.

"Now I [Joshua] *am about to go the way of all the earth. You know with all your heart and soul that* not one *of all the good promises the Lord your God gave you has failed.* Every *promise has been fulfilled;* not one *has failed"* (Joshua 23.14).

If anyone in the crowd could think of even one instance when God broke a promise, they would have corrected Joshua. "Uh, Josh, what about…?" But they didn't because none of God's promises failed; he kept every one. He never let them down.

But you don't have to take Joshua's word for it. Or Elijah's or Abraham's or anyone else you read about in the Bible. You have your own stories — all those times God came through for you, just as he promised.

If God's been faithful to you already, he'll be faithful again the next time you need to take a risk with nothing to go on except the character and promise of God. And that fact trumps all others.

Run with it:
When you find yourself in the widow's shoes and God asks you to take a risk, factor God and his promises into your decision-making process.

Remember, he didn't fail you before, and he won't fail you now.

DAY 8

The Blame Game

She said to Elijah, "What do you have against me, man of God? Did you come to remind me of my sin and kill my son?"
(1 Kings 17.18)

Read 1 Kings 17.17-24

Two men are marooned on a South Pacific Island. One guy is in a complete panic, pacing back and forth, ranting about how they're going to die and how no one will find them until they're nothing but bones. The other guy is snoozing peacefully on the beach.

The rattled guy marches up to him and screams, "What's wrong with you? Don't you understand the situation we're in?"

"Sure I do," he answers. "We're stranded on this island, hundreds of miles from anywhere."

"Aren't you worried?"

"Nope, I make 10,000 dollars a week."

At a complete loss, the first guy says, "What does that have to do with anything? You can't access it here, and there's no place to spend it even if you did."

To which the second guy replied, "No, you don't understand. I make 10,000 dollars a week and I tithe. My pastor will find me."

Bad things happen to everyone sometime. But like man #2, there's always a silver lining if we stop to look for it... even when it's hard to find.

The death of the widow of Zarephath's only son crushed her. She blamed God and angrily asked Elijah point-blank, *"Did you come to... kill my son?"* (1 Kings 17.18). How could she ignore God's goodness for more than a year with the never-ending supply of flour and oil? And yet, isn't that what we all do? In a moment of loss and suffering, we forget the blessings and constant love God showers on us. All his expressions of mercy and kindness and goodness, forgotten in the blink of an eye.

This tragedy was a double blow to the widow. Not only did she grieve as any mother who loses a child does, she also lost her only hope for the future. In her culture, a son was expected to provide for his mother in her old age. Now that's shattered. She bears the pain of her son's death and a future without a secure retirement plan she could count on.

So, she blames God and Elijah. Even Elijah doesn't understand why God put the widow through such pain. He's puzzled and wants an insight into God's thinking because the death of the boy didn't make sense to him, either.

God never does anything without a reason; there's always a purpose behind the pain. Sometimes he reveals his purpose to us. Other times, we must walk by faith with nothing to base it on other than the confidence our good God knows what he's doing, and it's for our best.

Job faced an accumulation of bad things. He endured dreadful suffering when tragedy after tragedy devastated his family and his business, and painful sores wracked his body. Job's story shows us it's possible for a man or a woman to endure intense agony without walking away from God. Keep two vital takeaways in mind the next time you find yourself in an unpleasant place:

- Job didn't know what was going on behind the scenes between God and Satan. Neither do you, but God controls it.
- Job didn't know how this chapter of his spiritual journey would turn out. Neither do you, but God writes it and his stories always have a happy ending.

When you go through seasons pockmarked with one terrible thing after another, remember God has a purpose for your pain. He has total control of what is going on in the background you're not privy to. Once God accomplishes his purpose, you'll see what he was up to and rejoice in what he did. You'll even tell him you'd go through it again to get those same benefits.

Elijah and the widow didn't have to wait long to discover what God was up to in the death of her son.

Elijah took the boy from his mother's arms, carried him up the stairs to his room, and laid him on his bed. Then he prayed a mere 11 words, *"O Lord my God, let this boy's life return to him"* (1 Kings 17.21), and God raised him from the dead!

What resulted from this tragedy? What was God's purpose behind the widow's pain? The boy was resurrected, and it's hard to imagine it didn't affect the direction of his life towards God. The news spread everywhere in the region, testifying to the presence and power of a God who can raise the dead. And the widow took another several steps closer to a relationship with God.

Awful things will come your way. That's a given. You can raise a clenched fist towards the heavens, or you can embrace them. You can run from God or run to God.

Whether you believe God has a wonderful purpose for your pain — even when you can't figure out what it is — will determine how you respond to it.

Run with it:

"Where has God come through for you? Really. Take a moment and remember. And then write it down. Remembering fertilizes our hope. It makes our faith burgeon and bloom. It strengthens our belief in the promises of God that he is good and he is for us. Remembering fuels our joy even when surrounded by thieves who want to steal it" (John Eldredge).

DAY 9
Into the Unknown

After a long time, in the third year, the word of the Lord came to Elijah: "Go and present yourself to Ahab, and I will send rain on the land."
(1 Kings 18.1)

Read 1 Kings 18.1-2

A historic mariner's chart drawn in 1525 sets on display in the British Museum in London. It outlines the North American coastline and its adjacent waters. The cartographer made some interesting notations on areas of the map that represented regions not yet explored.

He wrote: "Here be giants," "Here be fiery scorpions," and "Here be dragons."

The map came into the possession of Sir John Franklin, a British explorer in the early 1800s. He scratched out the fearful inscriptions and wrote, "HERE BE GOD" across the map.

Like the cartographer and Sir Franklin, people can see the same thing and come to different conclusions. Moses sent 12 spies to scope out the Promised Land before Israel invaded. The spies returned and reported the land was good, and there were powerful enemies they'd have to defeat in battle.

But that's where the agreement ended. Ten of the spies counseled against attacking the inhabitants of the land; two said without reservation they should fight for the land because God had promised it to them.

One set of facts; two interpretations. The unknown always does that to us.

Elijah is about to step into the unknown as we move into chapter 18 of 1 Kings. God protected him from King Ahab and fed him at the brook and later as a guest of the widow of Zarephath.

For three and one-half years, God kept him safe even as Ahab and Jezebel turned over every stone they could while searching for him. Maybe Elijah watched himself on John Walsh's television program, "Israel's Most Wanted." According to 1 Kings 18.10, Ahab looked in every nation and kingdom for him but came up empty every time. Now God tells Elijah to come out of hiding and present himself to Ahab.

Elijah — true to his character — obeys. Makes you wonder what you'd do in Elijah's shoes, doesn't it? Obey, or rationalize your disobedience?

Remember, Elijah was a normal person like you and me (James 5.17), so it's safe to assume he had conflicting emotions about meeting Ahab.

[1] *Fear.*

The unknown is always scary. God gave Elijah two things — a command: *"Go and present yourself to Ahab"* and a message: *"I will send rain on the land"* (1 Kings 18.1). That's all Elijah knew. God didn't tell him what Ahab would do. He doesn't know if God will continue to protect him or if it's the end. It's understandable Elijah is afraid.

BUT Elijah didn't let fear snuff out obedience. Even though he was scared, he still obeyed and went (1 Kings 18.2). The same way you should. Don't let fear choke out obedience to God. Do what God tells you to do, even if you must do it scared.

[2] *Faith.*

It's undeniable Elijah believed in God. Otherwise, he wouldn't have taken that first step in Ahab's direction, or those that followed. He rooted his faith in the promises, power, and prior performance of God. He'd already seen God do what he said he'd do — stop the rain, order ravens to bring him bread at the brook, keep the widow supplied with flour and oil. Amazing faith builders.

Based on God's faithfulness, Elijah concluded God would show up in power now, as he always had before. So he let faith win out over fear, and he went to see Ahab.

[3] *Anticipation.*

Stanley Jones wrote, "Many live in dread of what is coming. Why should we? The unknown puts adventure into life; it gives us something to sharpen our souls on.

The unexpected around the corner gives a sense of anticipation and surprise. If we saw all the good things which are coming to us, we would sit down and degenerate. If we saw all the evil things, we would be paralyzed. How merciful God is to lift the curtain on today, then slowwwwly lift the curtain on tomorrow."

Can't you imagine the sense of adventure and anticipation Elijah felt as he packed up to leave the widow and present himself to Ahab? "What's God got up his sleeve this time? I can't wait to see!" What a faith-inspired perspective on an unknown future.

At the very least, Elijah expected another demonstration of the Lord God's power and superiority when the promised rain fell. At best, he looked forward to a national revival and whole-hearted return to God.

David lived expecting amazing things from God, too. *"In the morning, O Lord, you hear my voice; in the morning I lay my requests before you and wait in expectation"* (Psalm 5.3).

How cool if you went through your day expecting all the things you'll get to see God do, rather than being anxious and fearful about the what ifs.

Run with it:

Whatever unknown future you face — the doctor's diagnosis tomorrow, losing a job, the call from the police department in the middle of the night, or any of a hundred other possibilities — scratch out anxiety, fear, and stress and write "HERE BE GOD" over the unknown.

DAY 10

Obedience is a Big Deal to God

So Elijah went to present himself to Ahab.
(1 Kings 18.2)

Read 1 Kings 18.1-2

A passenger in a taxi tapped the driver on the shoulder to ask him a question. The driver screamed, lost control of the cab, almost hit a bus, drove over the curb, and stopped inches from a large plate-glass window.

For a few moments, there was dead silence in the cab as each of the men imagined far worse scenarios. Then, the shaking driver said, "Are you OK? I'm so sorry, but you scared the daylights out of me."

The dazed passenger apologized to the driver and said, "I didn't realize that a mere tap on the shoulder would be such a big deal."

The driver replied, "No, no, I'm the one who is sorry. It's my fault. Today is my first day driving a cab. The previous 25 years, I drove a hearse."

A tap on the shoulder shouldn't be such a big deal. In fact, most of the things we think are a big deal aren't.

Most of the things we consider a big deal fall into the "doesn't matter" category. But some things are a big deal because they matter.

To God, watching his children obey him is a big deal. Obedience matters. It can mark the difference between a life that counts and one that is wasted. Elijah got the memo and took it to heart. We can sum up Elijah's life in two words: He *prayed* and he *obeyed*.

To this point, we've seen Elijah obey when he told Ahab God would withhold the rain. He obeyed when he moved to the brook, and again when the brook dried up and God sent him to Zarephath to stay with a widow.

Now God orders Elijah to do something that could cost him his life — present himself to Ahab. The same Ahab who had searched high and low for Elijah for over three years to get rid of him. But Elijah had developed a habit of obedience to God's commands.

"So Elijah went to present himself to Ahab" (1 Kings 18.2). Stated so matter-of-factly. God told him to go, he went. End of story. No matter the danger it presented. What happened after he obeyed was God's business. Elijah would obey and leave the outcome to God.

Obedience is a big deal to God. He blesses and works through those who obey him. Those who don't handcuff God from blessing them or working through them.

Take King Saul, Israel's first king, for example. From day one, Saul looked like a king and fought like a warrior who couldn't be beaten. But he had a flaw — he had a hard time doing what God told him to do if he had a better idea. His obedience was conditional.

The prophet Samuel came to him one day and told him to attack the Amalekites, and *"Totally destroy everything that belongs to them. Do not spare them; put to death men and women, children and infants, cattle and sheep, camels and donkeys"* (1 Samuel 15.3).

The orders from God seemed abhorrent to Saul. Unnecessary brutality. But his was not to give the orders; his was to obey them. God had his reasons, even if Saul couldn't figure them out. His sole responsibility was to obey the command.

Saul led his army into battle and defeated the Amalekites. He did what God told him to do... almost. He didn't kill Agag, their king, and he didn't kill the best of the animals. Bottom line, he didn't obey God. Samuel delivered a devastating message to Saul: *"You have rejected the word of the Lord, and the Lord has rejected you as king over Israel"* (1 Samuel 15.26).

Obedience is a big deal to God. So is disobedience.

It's still a big deal to God in the twenty-first century.

Samuel's words to King Saul echo through the ages: *"To obey is better than sacrifice, and to heed is better than the fat of rams"* (1 Samuel 15.22). God wants your obedience more than he wants your worship. But then, any worship is empty worship if God is not the King of our hearts, the one who calls the shots and we obey.

Samuel said more we dare not miss. *"For rebellion is like the sin of divination, and arrogance like the evil of idolatry"* (1 Samuel 15.23).

God sees disobedience as rebellion and arrogance. Rebellion is reserving for yourself the right to make the final decision on a matter. It's a declaration, "I have ultimate authority." You may weigh the pros and cons, but you get final say whether you'll obey them.

Arrogance is thinking you're smarter than God. That you know better than God what you should do. It's idolatry because you ascend the throne as God. Such foolishness and peril.

In Great Britain, citizens honor the king and queen as the rulers of the land, sovereigns before whom all bow in respect. But they are mere figureheads. Parliament runs the show. They are the actual rulers. It's Parliament that passes the laws all British citizens must obey.

Have you made God like the king and queen of England? Do you have the final say whether you obey God, or does he? Is he merely a figurehead, or is he indeed the King of your life with the authority to issue orders you must obey?

How you answer these questions is a big deal to God. It should be to you as well.

Run with it:

Take a moment for a personal assessment. Do you obey God no matter what, or only when you want to?

DAY 11

A Godly Man in an Ungodly Culture

While Jezebel was killing off the Lord's prophets, Obadiah had taken a hundred prophets and hidden them in two caves... and supplied them with food and water.
(1 Kings 18.4)

Read 1 Kings 18.1-18

Tom attended the same church as Ahmad, who had been a Muslim before Jesus transformed his life. After church one Sunday, Tom approached him and asked how he became Christian.

"When I lived in Madagascar, some British soldiers witnessed to me and I became convinced to give my life to Jesus," he said with a warm smile.

"What line of reasoning persuaded you to turn from Islam to the Christian faith?"

"It wasn't what they said, it was who they were, and how they lived their lives," he replied.

The power of a silent witness. The man or woman who quietly, but effectively, reflects the love and lifestyle of Jesus. A believer who bucks the tide of an anti-God culture, yet still attracts staunch unbelievers to Jesus by how they live.

Immorality and the worship of false gods made the years of Ahab's reign one of the lowest periods in Israel's history. But God was not without a witness.

There was the bold, brash, fearless Elijah who made life uncomfortable for the royal couple. And there was Obadiah, a quiet, unassuming follower of the Lord God who let his actions do the talking for him.

Whereas Elijah confronted Ahab, Obadiah never stood up to the king. He wasn't vocal about his faith like Elijah, but he wasn't afraid to let anyone see his devotion to God. Even in a culture in which he was part of a small minority, he resisted being swept up in the tide of Baal worship.

Elijah worked as an outsider; Obadiah as an insider who was a valued employee of King Ahab. His attitude, work ethic, trustworthiness, and commitment to excellence earned him promotion to overseer of the palace where he could be a godly presence amid all the evil around him. He found favor with the king despite being his polar opposite — Obadiah, a devoted lover of God, and Ahab, a staunch God-hater.

Obadiah's parents taught him the Lord God was the one true God, and the only God worthy of his worship. As an adult, he remained steadfast in his faith, being described as *"a devout believer in the Lord"* (1 Kings 18.3). He refused to be swept up in the popular movement toward Baal. He stood in stark contrast to those in the palace and on the street.

Jezebel initiated a campaign to exterminate every prophet of God and silence them. She fumed every time they charged her as a sinner and traitor to God. At great danger, Obadiah whisked 100 of God's prophets to safety, hiding them in two caves and supplying them with food and water. He couldn't save every prophet in the nation, but he did what he could.

Obadiah let his light shine in a very dark and godless culture. He said little, but his presence and the way he lived his life influenced those around him. He represented the Lord God to a nation who wanted nothing to do with God. Without a mega horn or a podcast or many allies or a political action committee, his impact on his generation pointed them to the one true God.

Does the way you live your life influence your generation for God?

Our culture is as wicked and God-hating as Obadiah's. Abortion, violent crime, racism, and sex trafficking are a blight on our nation. Physical, verbal, and sexual abuse in the home destroys families and wounds children for the rest of their lives. Corruption in government is on the rise. Intolerance and the cancel culture silence and divide. Anti-God curriculum taught in our schools brainwashes America's children with anti-Christian values and viewpoints. Churches increasingly compromise the clear teaching of the Word of God to fit in with culture.

It feels like we're beating our heads against a wall and losing ground everywhere we look, just like Elijah and Obadiah must have felt. But they never gave up or gave in. They steadfastly loved the Lord God and refused to follow the crowd or let it influence them.

Obadiah shows us it's possible to live a godly life in an anti-God culture of utter evil. And you don't have to be a Billy Graham to make a difference. Let's review how Obadiah did it:

- He stayed true to the faith his parents planted in him as a child.
- He let his devotion to God impact every area of his life.
- He worked with all his heart as an employee of Ahab because he recognized he was serving God, not man. That's why his attitude, commitment to excellence, faithfulness, and work ethic impressed wicked King Ahab.
- He courageously did all he could to help fellow believers. He couldn't save every prophet, but he did for some what he wanted to do for all.
- He let the God he loved, worshiped, and obeyed shine out of him like a lighthouse, and others saw God in him.
- He consistently obeyed God even though he didn't see the results he hoped for.

That's how Obadiah did it. You can do it the same way.

***Run with it*:**
Scan the bullet points that catalogue how Obadiah lived a godly life in an ungodly culture. Do you see anything on the list too hard for you to do? If not, your next steps are obvious.

DAY 12

Gotta Choose

*Elijah went before the people and said, "How long will you waver between two opinions? If the Lord is God, follow him; but if Baal is God, follow him."
But the people said nothing.*
(1 Kings 18.21)

Read 1 Kings 18.16-21

During World War II, Winston Churchill had to make a painful decision. One he couldn't avoid or pass off to someone else. He, and he alone, had to choose.

The British secret service broke the Nazi code and informed Churchill the Germans intended to bomb Coventry. He had two alternatives:

(1) Evacuate the citizens of Coventry and save hundreds of lives, at the expense of letting the Germans know they had broken the code.

(2) Take no action, which would kill hundreds of the citizens of Coventry, but keep the Nazi information flowing and save many more lives.

Churchill had to choose and he picked the second option.

Not all choices are as tough as Churchill's. Most of our choices fall into the "what am I going to make for supper, should I mow the lawn today, where should we go on vacation this summer" category. Sort of important, but not world-shattering.

But some choices shape our lives and the lives of others for years, even generations, to come. That's the kind of the choice Elijah insisted the people of Israel make. Choose God or Baal. You can't ride the fence any longer. You gotta choose.

But the people refused. They stood with eyes glued to the ground in utter silence except for the shuffling of feet and nervous clearing of throats. They wanted both Baal and God.

Israel was like an unfaithful partner in a marriage who doesn't want to divorce their spouse or give up their illicit lover. They want to keep both for the excitement of sex on the side, coupled with the security and comfort of marriage.

Every marriage partner has a legitimate claim to the *exclusive* love and commitment of their spouse. So does God. He isn't interested in divided loyalty. He demands undivided commitment and devotion.

Too many Christians haven't made up their minds. They want God to be a big *part* of their lives, but not their one and only. They want other gods on the side just in case. Jesus pointed out, *"You cannot serve both God and _____"* (Matthew 6.24). One will always take supremacy over the other. If the Lord God isn't your choice, another god is and it will be where you turn as your first resort when you're in need.

This tug-of-war for which God to choose dates to the Garden of Eden and the first lie about God ever targeted at mankind. *"God knows that when you eat of the tree, your eyes will be opened, and you will be like God, knowing good and evil"* (Genesis 3.5).

"God conned you," hissed the serpent. "He's holding out on you. He doesn't want to give you the things you need to be happy and fulfilled. You gotta go get it yourself."

Like Adam and Eve, we've bought into the lie and try to mix a pinch of God with a variety of substitute gods. These other gods give us just enough of a "high" we believe we need them. In the words of Kyle Idleman, we become "like the dog who drinks out of the toilet bowl and says, 'It doesn't get much better than this!'"

These stand-in gods are impotent impostors, unable to comfort us, relieve stress, change hearts or circumstances, give us hope or peace, strengthen us when we're weary, walk with us through the fires of adversity and testing, or satisfy the deepest longings of our soul. At best, they provide counterfeit remedies that are short-term and leave us no better off than when we turned to them.

You don't need "God and." God is all you need. He's always enough and always will be. Hear the testimony from those who've chosen God: *"No one whose hope is in you will ever be put to shame"* (Psalm 25.3). God has never disappointed those who chose him as their God, and you won't be the first.

The problem is we've drunk toilet water so long, we can't imagine God has anything better to offer. What a bunch of hooey from *"Satan, who leads the whole world astray"* (Revelation 12.9).

Elijah's voice echoes down the corridors of time: *"How long are you going to sit on the fence? If God is the real God, follow him; if it's Baal, follow him. Make up your minds!"* (1 Kings 18.21, MSG).

Even if you don't consciously pick who or what you'll worship, you will choose a god to run to when you're in trouble, either on purpose or by default. Referencing those who rejected God as their object of worship, Paul wrote, *"they worshiped and served created things rather than the Creator* (Romans 1.25). You will worship created things or the Creator who *"will take care of everything you need"* (Philippians 4.19, MSG) — physically, emotionally, mentally, and spiritually.

Dear reader, it's time to get off the fence. You gotta choose.

"When the author walks onto the stage, the play is over. God is going to invade, all right; but what is the good of saying you are on His side then... It will be too late then to choose your side. That will not be the time for choosing; it will be the time when we discover which side we really have chosen whether we realized it before or not. Now, today, this moment, is our chance to choose the right side" (C.S. Lewis).

***Run with it*:**
In the words of Joshua, *"Choose this day whom you will serve"* (Joshua 24.15). You gotta choose every new day.

DAY 13
Prove It

Then you call on the name of your god, and I will call on the name of the Lord. The god who answers by fire — he is God.
(1 Kings 18.24)

Read 1 Kings 18.22-29

In 2014, a group of consumers sued Red Bull, an energy drink, for false advertising. The company claimed, via their slogan, "Red Bull gives you wings," that their caffeinated drink would improve a consumer's concentration and reaction speed.

Beganin Caraethers was one of several consumers who sued the company. He said for 10 years he drank lots of Red Bull, but he had not developed "wings," or shown any signs of improved intellectual or physical abilities.

Advertising is a staple of American commerce. It's so big the federal government established the Better Business Bureau and the Federal Trade Commission. Their duty is to monitor the truthfulness of advertisements so consumers aren't duped into buying products that don't do what they claim to do.

Elijah launched the first Better Business Bureau on Mt. Carmel to investigate the truthfulness of the publicity Baal received. Ahab, Jezebel, and the prophets of Baal boasted Baal was God. Elijah disputed their claim and confronted them: "You advertise Baal is the all-powerful God who deserves the worship and adoration of everyone in Israel. Prove it!"

So Elijah dared Baal's prophets to a side-by-side comparison between their god and his God to prove which one performed as advertised. Consumers like side-by-side comparisons to learn which product performs better so they don't waste their hard-earned money on inferior merchandise.

Elijah laid out the parameters for the contest between God and Baal. Each side would choose a bull, cut it into pieces, and put it on a pile of wood. Neither Elijah nor the prophets of Baal could ignite their sacrifice. They must call upon their god to send fire, and the one who answered would prove he was the true and undisputed God.

The Israelites shouted their approval, backing the prophets of Baal into a corner. It's time to put up or shut up. They would either prove Baal is God and Israel should follow him, or expose him as a fraud and they should follow the Lord God of Elijah.

Baal's reputation had already taken a hit three-and-one-half years earlier when he, the god who his followers believed controlled the weather, couldn't undo God's decree there would be no rain until he said so. After

Elijah exposed that chink in his reputation, Baal must come through this time.

Elijah stepped aside and gave the prophets of Baal first shot and all the advantages. He gave them first dibs on the bull they wanted and let them go first to call upon Baal to send fire and consume their sacrifice. Baal must prove he was as advertised — the god above all gods who deserved the worship of the Israelites.

The prophets of Baal began their appeal to Baal at daybreak and continued until noon. *"But there was no response; no one answered"* (1 Kings 18.26). Elijah taunted them and ridiculed Baal. He wondered aloud if Baal was sleeping and needed awakened. Perhaps he was on vacation or was in the bathroom relieving himself.

His mocking insults whipped Baal's prophets into a desperate frenzy for three more hours. They shouted louder, danced wildly, and even cut themselves to get Baal's attention. *"But there was no response, no one answered, no one paid attention"* (1 Kings 18.29).

It's always like that with God-substitutes. They never live up to the hype or deliver what they promise. It's their slick advertising that hooks us. They guarantee happiness, fame, success, fulfillment, and the best of everything. But when we buy into their propaganda, they always leave us unsatisfied and disappointed.

When a product doesn't live up to its advertising, we don't buy it again. We look for one that does what it says it will do. But we don't do that with our God-substitutes. We give them endless chances. And even when they come up short again and again, we give them more chances, assuming the previous letdowns were a fluke and they'll come through next time.

God advertises a better "product" — living water that quenches your soul's thirst.

"Come, all you who are thirsty, come to the waters; and you who have no money, come buy and eat! Come buy wine and milk without money and without cost. Why spend money on what is not bread, and your labor on what does not satisfy? Listen, listen to me, and eat what is good, and your soul will delight in the richest of fare" (Isaiah 55.1-2).

Someone compiled the Seven Core Desires and Longings every person wants met: attention, affection, acceptance, affirmation, significance, satisfaction, and security. They're what you thirst for, aren't they?

So ask yourself: When I crave to experience one of the Seven Core Longings, do my God-substitutes quench my thirst, or do they leave me unsatisfied?

Then why do you cling to your God-substitutes and hold the Lord God at arm's length? Why do you reach for a Mt. Dew when God offers you a glass of sparkling, thirst-quenching, soul-satisfying living water? The Lord God is as advertised… unlike your God-substitutes.

Run with it:

It's obvious what you need to do — dump your Mt. Dew and go to God every time you're thirsty. Give some thought to that today, won't you?

DAY 14
Nothing is too Hard for God

Then the fire of the Lord fell and burned up the sacrifice, the wood, the stones and the soil, and also licked up the water in the trench.
(1 Kings 18.38)

Read 1 Kings 18.30-40

Bob Stacy often said, "I thought God could do the impossible, so I never put a limit on it."

During the 1960s, Stacy scratched out on a napkin a dream of a ministry to youth. It would be a huge undertaking, but he confidently set out to make his dream come true based on his firm belief he would never limit the God who does the impossible.

In 1968, Stacy launched Christ in Youth (CIY). He added staff and by 1970, they held their first youth conference. Over the next 50 years, CIY pursued Stacy's dream and created summer conferences for middle school, junior high school, and high school students, conferences, tools and curriculum for youth leaders, and international mission trips for young people to 12 countries.

Bob Stacy believed nothing was too hard for God, and he acted on his faith. He knew God can do anything, even what seems impossible.

That's what Elijah believed and practiced on Mt. Carmel when he challenged the prophets of Baal to prove their god deserved to be worshiped rather than the Lord God (1 Kings 18.20-39). Given first shot, Baal didn't live up to his press clippings. The Israelites saw him, perhaps for the first time, as an impotent fraud who couldn't send fire upon the sacrifice.

After the prophets of Baal embarrassed themselves, Elijah took his turn to prove to Israel beyond any doubt the God he followed was the one true God. A God who can do the impossible. The God they should give their complete allegiance and worship to.

So Elijah set up his altar and laid his bull on it. He dug a trench around the altar as the Israelites and prophets of Baal scratched their heads, wondering what he was up to. Then he dumped 12 large jugs of water on the wood. The water saturated the bull, the wood, and the altar and filled the trench. It would have been enough for Elijah to ask God to do what Baal couldn't and send fire on a dry sacrifice, but he wanted to leave no room for anyone to wonder who the true God was.

In case you were home sick the day your grade-school teacher taught the lesson on fire and water: water prevents fire from starting and puts it out once it's burning. Maybe Elijah missed the class too because he believed it wasn't any harder for God to ignite wood saturated with gallons of water than it was for him to set dry wood on fire.

After all, nothing is impossible for God.

In contrast to the frantic cries and gyrations of Baal's prophets, Elijah calmly and confidently prayed. *"O Lord, God of Abraham, Isaac and Israel, let it be known today that you are God in Israel... Answer me, O Lord, answer me, so these people will know that you, O Lord, are God, and that you are turning their hearts back again"* (1 Kings 18.36-37).

A simple prayer. A prayer that took less than 30 seconds to pray. Elijah barely finished before the Lord hurled down fire from the sky and burned up the bull, the wood, the stones, and the soil, and licked up all the water in the trench.

Game, set, match. God wins!

The people who shied away from choosing between Baal and the Lord God only hours earlier no longer wavered. Dazzled by such a display of power, the Israelites burst into deafening shouts, "The Lord, he is God! The Lord, he is God!" Their roars shook the mountain and removed their doubts.

This was not the first time God proved it was a snap for him to do the impossible. God packed the Bible with evidence. A 100-year-old woman gave birth to a baby as God promised her husband, Abraham. A virgin gave birth to the Messiah. God parted the waters of the Red Sea so his people escaped the advancing Egyptian army resolute on butchering them. He collapsed the walls of

Jericho after Joshua led an Israelite hike around it for seven days. He raised Lazarus from the dead.

For God, anything is possible. Nothing is too hard for him. Nothing can stop him or slow him down. There isn't anything he can't do

The God of Elijah still does what he's always done.

- Heal any disease
- Mend any hurt
- Break the hold of any addiction or habit
- Restore hope crushed by despair
- Bring the prodigal son, daughter, father, or mother home
- Repair a broken marriage that seems beyond fixing
- Open doors that are closed
- Impart strength for the hardest trial
- Soften the hardest heart
- Reconcile fractured relationships
- Replace anxiety with peace, and depression with joy

Nothing is impossible for God. Nothing is too hard for him.

Remember that the next time you're in a pinch and need a miracle.

Run with it:

Consider a difficulty you're facing. Now write it in the blank: Is _____ too hard for God?

DAY 15

Relentless

"... that you are turning their hearts back again."
(1 Kings 18.37)

Read 1 Kings 18.37

Clint Courtney was never an All-Star and didn't expect to be inducted into the Baseball Hall of Fame. He wasn't speedy on the base paths and didn't hit for power, but he was a tough catcher.

Often doubled over in agony from foul tips and collisions at home plate, Courtney never quit. He'd get up, shake off the dust, punch the pocket of his mitt once or twice, and nod to his pitcher to throw another one. The game continued, and Courtney, bloodied, bruised, and in pain, doggedly took his position behind the plate for another inning.

Clint Courtney provides a picture of God's persistence. God never gives up, no matter how many times his creation rejects him. His pursuit of unbelievers and half-hearted Christians is relentlessness.

We get a snapshot of God's unrelenting pursuit in the contest on Mt. Carmel. He never abandoned Israel despite centuries when they replaced him with countless counterfeit gods. God sent Elijah to turn their hearts back to him even after Ahab had tried to eliminate every trace of him from Israel.

Elijah's prayer (1 Kings 18.37) revealed a two-fold objective at the Battle of the Gods on Mt. Carmel: [a] prove the Lord God was the true God and [b] proclaim God wanted his people back. He hadn't given up on them or removed his love from them.

It's a theme repeated on almost every page of the Bible. No matter what you've done, God wants you back. Regardless how far you've run from him, God wants you back. Despite how many times you've turned to counterfeit gods instead of him, God wants you back.

"This is God who, when turned down, ignored, rejected — even violently, even blasphemously — finds a new way to express his love and issue the invitation. This is a God who has never given up on winning your heart. Never" (Kyle Idleman).

That goes for the burden you carry for your family and friends who reject God's invitation to a life-giving relationship with him. He hasn't given up on them… and he never will. Take heart, he won't relent until he has their hearts. And yours.

For a believer who has strayed from God and an unbeliever whose heart is feeling God's tug, one of the biggest hurdles is their past. They can't believe after all they've done God would still want them. Still love them.

Still forgive them. Haven't they already crossed the line of no return?

Look at the story of the Prodigal Son. After realizing his mistake in rejecting his father's love for so many years, the son decides to return to his father. Wracked with shame and regret, he prepares a speech. *"Father, I have sinned... I am no longer worthy to be called your son; make me like one of your hired men"* (Luke 15.18-19).

Just like the prodigal, we find it hard to believe God wants anything to do with us after we've sinned, turned to lesser gods, and repented of a sin only to return to it again. At best, we hope if we work hard enough to be a good Christian, one day we can earn his love. Truth is, it's not about being good enough. It's the unbelievable truth that God has been calling you because he loves you and wants you back.

As the son gets closer and closer to home, his anxiety rises. What will his dad's response be? Will he tell him he's made his own bed, now go sleep in it? Will he turn his back on him and toss him out onto the street?

The father's response is unexpected. As soon as he spots his son in the distance, he sprints down the road to hug him and shower him with kisses. The son starts his speech, *"Father, I have sinned... I am no longer worthy to be called your son..."* (Luke 15.21), but his father cuts him off. He will have none of it. "You've sinned, yes, but you are still my son, no matter what you've done. I love you. I always have, and I always will. I'm so glad you're home."

Jason Michael Carroll wrote a song called "Hurry Home." It tells the story of a father whose daughter left home, vowing to never return. He sat by the phone one evening hoping for her to call. He grabbed his old guitar, turned on his answering machine, and crooned these words:

> It doesn't matter what you've done, I still love you
> It doesn't matter where you've been, you can still come home
> And honey, if it's you, we've got a lot of making up to do
> And I can't hug you on the phone, so hurry home

Years passed without a word from his daughter. Friends asked him if he thought it was time to take the message off his voicemail. He wouldn't do it because, who knows, she still might call.

One day, his daughter's friends betrayed her. Scared, alone, wounded, and weary, she decided it was time to call her dad. Afraid what his response would be, she punched in the numbers with trembling hands. Would be want her back? Would he hang up on her? The phone rang, and she got the answering machine. She cried as she listened to her dad sing the lyrics he'd written for her.

The father walked through his front door just in time to catch her say, "Dad, I'm on my way."

That's what your heavenly Father longs to hear from you. And he won't relent until you do.

***Run with it*:**
Ponder this today: God relentlessly pursues you, and he won't quit until you come home.

DAY 16

Let It Rain

And Elijah said to Ahab, "Go, eat and drink, for there is the sound of a heavy rain."
(1 Kings 18.41)

Read 1 Kings 18.41-46

In 1848, James W. Marshall found gold at Sutter's Mill launching the California Gold Rush. When word got out, 300,000 people from the United States and abroad traveled to California to seek their fortune.

Among them was a man from Ohio. He got a claim, bought the tools, and went to work. After several months of hard labor with no success, the Ohioan was tired, worn out, and discouraged. So he sold his claim and equipment to another miner with gold in his eyes.

A surveyor advised the new miner there was gold only three feet away from where the first miner stopped digging. The surveyor was right — the Ohioan was a mere three feet from striking gold. If only he hadn't given up because the work exhausted him, and he didn't see fast results.

Like the Ohioan, many Christians quit praying about something just before God is ready to move on their behalf. They're just "three feet away" from the answer, but they never see it because they give up too soon.

When did God ever promise a quick answer to our prayers?

We've adopted the notion that if God is going to act, he's going to act instantly. Bam. Zap. But that's not what we find in so many biblical accounts. Occasionally, God answers right away.

We've already seen swift answers to prayer three times in the life of Elijah. He prayed, and God prevented rainfall in an instant. God raised the widow's son immediately after Elijah prayed. On Mt. Carmel, Elijah barely finished his prayer before God sent fire and consumed his offering.

Let's not limit God's ability to answer our prayers quickly. At the same time, we must not expect swift answers to our every prayer. Those are the exceptions rather than the rule.

The fourth time we see Elijah pray, he asks God to send rain and end the three-plus years of drought. In contrast to the three prior times Elijah prayed, perseverance was required. Six times, he prayed and then sent his servant to spot rain heading their way. Six times, his servant returned and told him, *"There is nothing there"* (1 Kings 18.43). But on the seventh time, *"the sky grew black with clouds, the wind rose, and a heavy rain came"* (1 Kings 18.45).

Elijah didn't give up. He wouldn't take "no" for an answer. Previous experience had persuaded him God had the power to do what he had promised — send rain that very day (1 Kings 18.1). So, Elijah stubbornly continued to pray until the rain came.

God answers prayer, but most of the time you must pray the same prayer over and over, day after day. Persevering prayer shows God you're serious about what you're asking him. Your desire to get an answer from God drives you to persevere in prayer for as long as it takes.

John Eldredge observes, "Prayer is not just asking God to do something and waiting for him to zap it. Intervening prayer often takes time. And it takes repetition."

Cotton Mather prayed several hours a day for 20 years for revival. The Great Awakening sprang up the year after his death.

William Wilberforce prayed in secret and fought in Parliament for 55 years to abolish slavery in England and the British Empire. Parliament passed the law as he lay on his deathbed.

George Muller preserved an amazing portrait of persistent prayer in his journal:

"In November 1844, I began to pray for the conversion of five individuals. I prayed every day without a single intermission, whether sick or in health, on the land or on the sea, and whatever the pressure of my engagements might be.

"Eighteen months elapsed before the first was converted. I thanked God and prayed on for the others. Five years elapsed and the second was converted. I thanked God for the second and prayed on for the other three. Day by day I continued to pray for them, and six years passed before the third was converted. I thanked God for the three and went on praying for the other two. These two remained unconverted.

"The man [Muller] to whom God in the riches of his grace has given tens of thousands of answers to prayer in the self-same hour or day in which they were offered has been praying day by day for nearly 36 years for the conversion of these individuals, and yet they remain unconverted. But I hope in God, I pray on, and look yet for the answer. They are not converted yet, *but they will be*."

Muller's faith in the promises of God constrained him to pray daily for another 16 years for the last two men, and God saved both of them after he died.

Are you getting the picture? God looks for believers who will pray his will and keep at it until he answers.

Run with it:

A promise from Jesus to you — *Keep on asking, and you will receive what you ask for. Keep on seeking, and you will find. Keep on knocking, and the door will be opened to you* (Matthew 7.7).

DAY 17

Roots of Depression

*Elijah was afraid and ran for his life…
and prayed that he might die.*
(1 Kings 19.3-4)

Read 1 Kings 19.1-4

In 1835, a man deep in the clutches of depression visited a doctor in Florence, Italy. He couldn't eat or sleep, and he avoided his friends.

The doctor examined him and found no physical cause for his condition. He concluded the man needed something to lift his spirits. The physician informed his patient a circus was in town and its star performer, a clown named Grimaldi, was sure to pull him out of his depression.

"Night after night he has people rolling in the aisles," the doctor said. "Grimaldi is the world's funniest clown. He'll make you laugh and cure your sadness. You must go see him."

"No," replied the despairing man. "He can't help me. I am Grimaldi!"

Sometimes the person you least expect to be depressed finds himself in that dark pit. Whether you're a world-famous clown who makes others laugh, or a prophet of God.

Elijah should be on the highest high he's ever experienced. He'd exposed Baal as the fake he was, set the stage for a major revival, and rain fell at last. Instead he found himself on Jezebel's most wanted list, and the spiritual awakening had already fizzled out.

Elijah *"was afraid and ran for his life"* (1 Kings 19.3). Powered by fear, disappointment, and discouragement, Elijah fled 80 miles to Beersheba to dodge Jezebel. He spied a broom tree with its low branches providing shelter from the intense sun and snooping eyes. Then he prayed. *"I have had enough, Lord. Take my life; I am no better than my ancestors"* (1 Kings 19.4).

Elijah felt he couldn't do it anymore. The work was stressful and exhausting. There wasn't any fruit from his efforts. The victory on Mt. Carmel didn't result in the nation turning to God as he imagined. Like the prophets before him, Elijah pointed out sin, called Israel to repentance, and reminded them God wanted them back, but with negligible results. Elijah was a results-oriented guy, and when he didn't see any, it drove him to depression.

Spoiler Alert: Christians aren't immune from depression or other negative emotions. Every saint is susceptible to the wanna run/wanna quit response no matter how mature they are in Christ.

Elijah suffered depression because its roots found fertile soil in his mind.

Root #1 — *Unrealistic expectations.*

Elijah thought happy days would be here again after the great success on Mt. Carmel. Instead, Jezebel hunted him again, and he discovered hardened hearts that returned to their pre-Mt. Carmel behavior and worship of Baal.

Unrealistic expectations are creations of man, not rooted in a direct promise from God. They don't factor in the free-will of people to repent or to reject God. Elijah lacked a word from God that revival would result from his efforts, but he expected it anyway. When it didn't happen, it deposited him into the pits.

Whenever you have a goal that appears impossible and hopeless, depression is on the doorstep. Slam shut the door to your mind and don't let depression make itself at home. Remind yourself as often as you must that everything is possible with God even when all signs say otherwise. *"The one who calls you is faithful, and he will do it"* (1 Thessalonians 5.24).

Root #2 — *Faulty perspective.*

Because of the lack of results, Elijah concluded he was a failure. He'd given everything he had and nothing changed, so he was done.

What Elijah forgot is how God defines success. A believer is a success if he or she remains faithful to God and their assigned task, regardless of the results, setbacks, or challenges. Just stick with it. *"Now it is required that those who have been given a trust must prove faithful"* (1 Corinthians 4.2).

God's message to Elijah and to you is: Be faithful. Do what I tell you to do. Don't back down and don't quit. Leave the results to me. That's my job.

Root #3 — *Isolation.*

Elijah left his servant in Beersheba and went into the desert alone. Beware of isolation! It's one of the worst things you can do when you're depressed or teetering on the brink of depression.

When you detach yourself from others, you have no one to encourage you; no one to remind you of the truth; no one to pray with you; no one to speak into your soul; no one to help you see clearly; no one to point out your expectations are unrealistic and your perspective is off; no one to tell you it's not as bad as you think it is; no one to remind you it won't always be like this.

"Two are better than one, because they have a good return for their work: If one falls down, his friend can help him up. But pity the man who falls and has no one to help him up! Though one may be overpowered, two can defend themselves" (Ecclesiastes 4.9-10, 12).

God stood ready to help Elijah find a way out of depression. *"He reached down from on high and took hold of me; he drew me out of deep waters"* (Psalm 18.16). He's ready to help you, too.

***Run with it*:**
Pause to check if you've fallen victim to unrealistic expectations, a skewed perspective, and/or isolation. If you have, recenter your thoughts on God and his Word.

DAY 18
A Way Out of Depression

*There he went into a cave and spent the night. And the
word of the Lord came to him:
"What are you doing here, Elijah?"*
(1 Kings 19.9)

Read 1 Kings 19.3-14

A man phoned a pastor in his town and said, "I want to make you aware of a family who is in terrible need. Both parents are out of work and struggling to make ends meet. They have six children, and they're going to be evicted from their home unless someone pays $3000 in back rent they owe."

"Oh, my!" the pastor said. "I'll see what we can do. May I ask who you are?"

"I'm their landlord."

Now that's initiative, like God took with Elijah. After Jezebel threatened his life, Elijah bolted to Beersheba in fear and succumbed to depression. His unrealistic expectations and distorted perspective dragged him into a dark hole where he sunk so low he wanted to die.

God initiated an intervention to help Elijah out of the pit. Counter to the way most people view God when they mess up, God didn't lecture him, shame him, rebuke him, question his faith, make him feel like Elijah disappointed him, or give him logical reasons why his depression was invalid.

Beating up a depressed person or telling him to snap out of it doesn't help because it doesn't work. If Elijah could tell himself to stop feeling depressed, he would have done it already. But you can't stop depression by decree because feelings (positive or negative) resist the will. To change your feelings, you must control what you think about because your thoughts determine your feelings. If you think depressed thoughts, you'll get depressed.

That's where Elijah was, so God made the first move to lend a hand up out of the pit of depression. But before he could deal with Elijah's thoughts, he had to deal with other issues first.

[1] ***Rest***

Elijah was physically, emotionally, and mentally exhausted after his 100-mile run and his disappointment in the outcome of the Mt. Carmel victory. He spotted a broom tree with its low-lying branches that provided shade from the burning sun and protection from prying eyes. He crawled under it and fell asleep (1 Kings 9.5). After he ate, he went back to bed (1 Kings 19.6).

"[Depression] all starts with not wanting to get out of bed," stated someone who battles depression.

God didn't disturb Elijah's rest. He gave him time to refresh and recharge because rest is an essential part of the pathway out of depression. Fatigue stands in the way of recovery.

[2] ***Proper nutrition***

What a depressed person eats either feeds their depression or helps lead them out of it. So between naps, God sent an angel to bring food to Elijah. After adequate sleep and a couple nutritional meals, he was *"strengthened by that food"* (1 Kings 19.8) and ready for the next step on his journey out of the pit of despair.

[3] ***Exercise***

Physical exercise and movement are critical weapons to combat depression. If allowed to follow their feelings, depressed people will stay in bed all day. But that only leads them deeper and deeper into darkness and gloom. Physical activity feeds recovery.

God wouldn't let Elijah stay inactive. He sent the angel again with another meal, and then sent him on a journey. Though he didn't want to go, Elijah obeyed. That's shocking because depressed people know what to do to get out of their depression, but they don't feel like doing it... so they don't. But Elijah got out of bed, ate some food, and began an "exercise program" that required him to walk 200 miles in 40 days and 40 nights to Mt. Horeb.

[4] ***Time***

God wasn't in a hurry to get Elijah back to work. He needed plenty of time to rest and sort things out, and that doesn't come quickly or easily. You can't rush recovery.

[5] ***Time alone with God***

While proper nutrition, rest, and exercise are important, the most valuable use of your time is to get alone with God. After Elijah arrived at Mt. Horeb and spent the night in a cave, God engaged him in a conversation (1 Kings 19.9-14). Before God could help him think straight, Elijah needed time to vent, a place to unload his frustrations and anger.

Elijah didn't tiptoe around God with disingenuous words. He didn't hide his true feelings. He was brutally honest and told God how he really felt with no filter.

But God didn't take offense. He didn't rain down fire and brimstone on him or strike him dumb. He listened to Elijah spill out all the ugliness in his soul. God took it and when Elijah was done, God spoke to him in a gentle, quiet whisper.

We find here two lessons.

One, you can tell God how you really feel. All of it. It's not like he doesn't know, anyway.

Two, you must pay attention to what God has to say to you. We'll delve into that in the next two devotionals.

***Run with it*:**
God cares about any emotion you struggle with and promises help. *"He lifted me out of the pit of despair, out of the mud and the mire. He set my feet on solid ground and steadied me as I walked along. He put a new song in my mouth, a hymn of praise to our God"* (Psalm 40.2-3).

DAY 19
Perspective

I have been very zealous for the Lord God Almighty. The Israelites have rejected your covenant, broken down your altars, and put your prophets to death with the sword. I am the only one left, and now they are trying to kill me too."
(1 Kings 19.14)

Read 1 Kings 19.11-18

Dear Mom and Dad,
Wanted to email you and tell what's going on with me. I've fallen in love with a guy named Jim. He quit high school after grade eleven to get married. About a year ago, he got a divorce. We've been going steady for two months and plan to get married in the fall. Until then, I've moved into his apartment (I think I might be pregnant). At any rate, I dropped out of school last week, but I hope to finish sometime.

(On an attachment to the email she wrote.)
Mom and Dad, I just want you to know that everything I've written so far in this letter is false. NONE of it is true. But Mom and Dad, it IS true that I got a C-

in French and flunked my math class... and it IS true that I'm going to need more money for my tuition payments.

Love, your daughter Sara.

Before dropping the bomb, Sara gave her parents perspective. Compared to the news in the attachment, the message in the email was great news. It's all a matter of perspective.

A skewed perspective is one of the largest contributors to negative emotions. As we've seen, it played a big role in Elijah's depression. God didn't want his prophet to suffer and wallow there, so he addressed five physical factors that feed depression: rest, diet, exercise, time, and an opportunity to unload his frustration and anger to God. (See Day 18 for details)

With the physical ingredients addressed, God offered Elijah three other ways out of his depression. Today, we'll focus on the first: *Change your perspective.*

When we're overwhelmed with fear or depression, we aren't thinking straight. Our perspective blinds us to reality, it messes with our faith, and it makes us forget God has everything under control.

When we have a distorted assessment of our situation, we end up believing things that aren't true, and that influences how we feel and how we see life… even if it's inaccurate.

Depression overwhelmed Elijah because he believed some untrue things. Even so, Elijah believed they were true and that's what changed him from a fearless prophet into a fearful fugitive. On Mt. Carmel, he boldly stood alone against King Ahab, the prophets of Baal, and the Israelites. A model of unwavering faith, but that's when his eyes were on God.

Now Elijah's perception was [a] Jezebel would kill him, [b] he wasn't accomplishing anything, and [c] he was all alone. His conclusions were wrong, yet they dictated his feelings and behavior.

The truth was [a] God would keep Elijah safe from Jezebel, [b] he was accomplishing what God wanted him to accomplish — to represent him and deliver his message, and [c] he was far from alone — there were the 100 prophets of God Obadiah had hidden (1 Kings 18.4), plus 7000 others who stood against the tide of Baal worship (1 Kings 19.18), and best of all, God himself stood with him.

Elijah held to his view rather than the truth, and it negatively affected him. The solution was to stop and look at his situation through God's eyes. To change his perspective.

Elisha, Elijah's successor, caused headaches for the king of Aram. He waged war against Israel, but Elisha exposed his every move to the king of Israel who took steps to thwart the enemy's tactics. The Aramean king sent a large contingent of horses, chariots, and troops to capture Elisha when he learned he was the culprit messing up his plans.

The next morning, Elisha's servant spotted the army surrounding the city. His take on the situation was they were doomed to death or arrest. He rushed to warn

Elisha, who told his servant, *"Don't be afraid. Those who are with us are more than those who are with them"* (2 Kings 6.16).

Same situation; opposite perspectives and thus different conclusions. Elisha perceived their circumstances from God's point of view. He prayed God would enable his servant to see what he did. *"Then the Lord opened the servant's eyes, and he looked and saw the hills full of horses and chariots of fire all around Elisha"* (2 Kings 6.17).

It's all about getting God's perspective on your situation and holding on to it, no matter what happens. To maintain the right outlook, you must remind yourself of a few unchanging truths.

- Things have not always been like they are now
- Things will not always be like they are now
- You're unaware about what God is doing behind the scenes
- You don't know the final chapter
- God is your refuge and strength, an ever-present help in times of trouble (Psalm 46)
- God has been faithful to you before; he will be faithful again

If these truths don't change your perspective, nothing will.

Run with it:

Jot the six truths above on an index card and reread them often. Let God's perspective replace yours.

DAY 20
A Task and a Friend

... and anoint Elisha son of Shaphat from Abel Meholah to succeed you as prophet.
(1 Kings 19.16)

Read 1 Kings 19.15-19

An efficiency expert concluded a lecture with a note of caution, "You don't want to try these techniques at home."

"Why not?" asked someone from the back of the audience.

"I watched my wife's routine at breakfast for years," the expert explained. "She made lots of trips to the refrigerator, stove, table, and cabinets, often carrying just a single item at a time. 'Honey,' I suggested, 'Why don't you try carrying several things at once?'"

The person in the audience asked, "Did it save time?"

The expert replied, "Actually, yes. It used to take *her* 20 minutes to get breakfast ready. Now *I* do it in seven."

Criticism rarely works. It's counter-productive, and the one criticized often feels worthless and quits. What's the point, they think, if I give my best effort and all I ever hear is I'm doing it wrong?

God takes a different approach. He lets us dump our rawest, most unfiltered feelings on him, and he just holds us and assures us everything will be okay. That's how he dealt with Elijah in his lowest moments. Because Elijah held unrealistic expectations after what happened on Mt. Carmel and viewed the future with a skewed perspective, fear assaulted him and depression took a death grip on him.

God kindly offered Elijah a blueprint to lift him out of the abyss that filled his mind with thoughts of hopelessness and defeat. In the last two devotionals, we examined six parts of God's plan to restore Elijah. Today we wrap it up with the final two.

God gave Elijah something to do.

When you're depressed, you don't feel like doing anything. You stay in bed or sit in a dark room that matches your mood. It becomes an escape, your place to hide, but it enables gloom to gain a stronger foothold on your heart and further distort your perspective.

God wouldn't allow Elijah to wallow in a pity party for long. He gave Elijah something to do (1 Kings 19.15-18). Doing something gets your eyes off yourself and begins the process of healing.

Sounds easy, but it isn't. There's a huge barrier to overcome — your emotions. Most of the time, we let them dictate our action. Even when the depressed knows completing an assignment will make them feel better, they rarely do it because they don't feel like it. If they don't feel like doing anything, nine times out of ten, they won't.

Elijah is proof that forcing yourself to do something when you don't feel like it makes a difference. He overruled his feelings and obeyed God, and the depression broke soon after. The old Elijah is back when we see him a couple of days later confront King Ahaziah (2 Kings 1).

God had one more recommendation to help Elijah... and you.

<u>God gave him a friend</u>.

We've seen the curse isolation was to Elijah. It deepens depression and hopelessness. It takes you out of the game where you watch the work of God from the sidelines. Going into seclusion is one of the worst things you can do when you find yourself in the pits.

So God gave Elijah a friend — Elisha. Elisha needed Elijah to mentor him and prepare him to succeed Elijah as prophet, but God didn't intend it to be a one-way street. Elijah needed Elisha as much as Elisha needed him.

Elijah needed a shoulder to cry on and someone who would be brutally honest with him. He needed a friend to help him keep his perspective focused on God and his faithfulness. Someone to push him to discipline himself to do what he needed to do, even when he didn't feel like it.

This isn't a new concept. Far from it. Go back to creation and you'll hear God say, "*it's not good for a man to be alone*," so he made a helper for him (Genesis 2.18).

Jesus gathered twelve men around him for more than discipleship. He needed a band of brothers, a few close friends to be at his side when he went through hard times.

Look at the lead-up to Calvary. He made his way to the Garden of Gethsemane where he poured out his heart to his Father. In desperation and surrender to God's will, he pled for strength to go through the agony he knew was hours away. He didn't want to be alone; he needed friends with him. So Jesus hand-picked Peter, James, and John, his three closest friends, to go with him during his biggest challenge in life (Matthew 26.37-38).

Francis Schaeffer observed, "Christianity is not a modern success story… If there seems to be no results, remember that Jeremiah did not see the results in his day. [*Neither did Elijah*.] They came later. If there seem to be no results, it does not change God's imperative. It is simply up to you and to me to go on, go on, go on, go on, whether we see the results or whether we don't. Go on" (*Death in the City*, page 75).

You can go on by yourself for short periods of time with no one to encourage you or work beside you, but not over the long haul. To remain steadfast and move ahead when results fall far short of expectations, you must have a circle of friends to support you.

Run with it:

A few close friends are imperative for your spiritual journey. Can you name two to four friends who will journey with you? If not, who might you cultivate that kind of relationship with?

DAY 21
A Whisper

After the earthquake came a fire, but the Lord was not in the fire. And after the fire came a gentle whisper.
(1 Kings 19.12)

Read 1 Kings 19.9-13

President Franklin Roosevelt despised the long receiving lines of foreign dignitaries and guests to the White House. He complained no one paid any attention to what anyone said. They smiled, shook hands, and spoke politely, but no one really listened.

During one reception, he experimented with his theory. To each person who passed down the line, he shook their hand and murmured, "I murdered my grandmother this morning."

The guests responded with phrases like, "Marvelous! Keep up the good work. We are proud of you. God bless you, sir."

Near the end of the line, the ambassador from Bolivia heard what Roosevelt said. Without batting an eye, he leaned forward and whispered, "I'm sure she had it coming, Mr. President."

Today, we find Elijah still weighed down with depression. He believes reality is what he sees and feels when it's really nothing but make-believe. He's so convinced death is around the corner and he's a total failure, he doesn't bring God into his situation or question whether his emotions are valid. He's not listening.

Since he fled Jezebel, God delivered his messages to Elijah through an angel, but not this time. It's as if God said, "Hey, Elijah, it's time we had a talk. Go stand on the mountain, I'm about to pass by." So Elijah obeyed and God came.

A powerful wind tore apart the mountain and shattered rocks, but God wasn't in it.

Next came an earthquake, but God wasn't in it, either.

Then fire appeared, but God wasn't in the fire.

"And after the fire came a gentle whisper... Then a voice said to him, 'What are you doing here, Elijah?'" (1 Kings 19.12-13).

We aren't privy to the way God spoke to Elijah. We don't know if it was an audible voice, a thought God planted in his mind, or something altogether different. But this time, it was just a still, small voice. A gentle whisper.

David uses the Hebrew word for whisper in Psalm 107.29, *"He stilled the storm to a whisper; the waves of the sea were hushed."* God knew his servant was in the throes of an inner storm, so he spoke in a gentle whisper to hush the waves.

For a person to hear God speak, at least three things must happen. They apply whether God speaks from the pages of the Bible as you read, or in an unmistakable impression he whispers to your heart or mind.

[1] *You gotta get close to God*.

You can't hear a whisper from a distance. You must get up close. It's difficult to make out a whisper in a crowded room with a cacophony of sound surrounding you. You must leave the noise and get alone. Moses set up a tent away from the busy commotion and racket of the Israelite camp where he could find a quiet place to be close to God without interruptions or distractions. Jesus often slipped away from the crowds and his disciples to a deserted place to talk with his Father.

If you want to find out what God wants to tell you, you must follow their example.

[2] *You gotta be still*.

You won't hear God amid the blare of the TV or radio in the background, or if your mind is racing 1000 miles per hour about money worries. You must get alone, slow down, close your eyes, take a deep breath, and quiet your mind. The Psalmist wisely advised, *"Be still and know I am God"* (Psalm 46.10). Relax. Take a few minutes to release the stress.

In the stillness, God can remind you he is your *"refuge and strength, an ever-present help in times of trouble"* (Psalm 46.1). Then you *"will not fear though the earth give way and the mountains fall into the heart of the sea"* (Psalm 46.2).

If you want to listen to God, you must quiet yourself and be still.

[3] *You gotta pay attention*.

If you want to perceive God's whisper, you must decide who will win the tug-of-war for your attention. People and things vie for it constantly. Your cluttered mind demands you heed its worries and what ifs. You can only give your full attention to one thing at a time, and you get to choose what gets that top spot.

When Jesus visited Mary and Martha at their home, they chose different things. Martha missed a conversation with Jesus because she decided fixing dinner for him and her other guests was the most important thing she could do right then. Mary decided to give her full attention to Jesus because he outweighed everything else competing for it. Jesus agreed, *"Martha, Martha, you are worried and upset about many things, but only one thing is needed. Mary has chosen what is better"* (Luke 10.41-42).

To tune-in to God's gentle whisper, you must put away everything that may distract you. Lay down the newspaper, turn off the TV, put away the video game controllers, move away from the dishes in the sink, set aside the project you're working on, let the grass and garden wait until later. The opportunity to hear God speak to you is more important than any of those activities.

Run with it:

God wanted to speak with Samuel, so he picked Eli to instruct him how to listen for God. Eli told him to say, "Speak, Lord, for your servant in listening." Try it yourself a few times this week.

DAY 22

The Cost of the Call

So Elijah went from there and found Elisha... Elijah went up to him and threw his cloak around him.
(1 Kings 19.19)

Read 1 Kings 19.19-21

Fifty-six men signed the Declaration of Independence aware it would cost them untold suffering for themselves and their families. Of the 56 men, The British captured and tortured five men before they died. Twelve had their homes ransacked and burned. Two lost their sons in battle. Another had two sons captured. Nine of the fifty-six fought in the war and died from wounds or hardships. Carter Braxton of Virginia, a wealthy planter and trader, saw his ships sunk by the British navy. He sold his home and properties to pay his debts and died in poverty.

Anything of real value will cost something. After Elijah carried out his assignment and anointed Elisha as his successor, Elisha had to weigh whether the call of God held greater value than giving up the comfort and security of home, family, and wealth.

The four fishermen Jesus called to leave behind their fishing nets and business to follow him had to evaluate which option carried the greatest benefit. They picked Jesus.

Moses had a similar decision to make. The writer of Hebrews spells it out: *"He chose to be mistreated along with the people of God rather than to enjoy the pleasures of sin for a short time. He regarded disgrace for the sake of Christ as of greater value than the treasures of Egypt because he was looking ahead to his reward"* (Hebrews 11.25-26).

Paul said yes to Jesus even though the personal cost was great. The price tag included prison, severe floggings, beatings, stoning, sleepless nights, betrayal, hunger and thirst, rejection, weariness, and loneliness.

Yet Paul considered all that worth it, so much so he called them *"light and momentary troubles"* because he saw them *"achieving for us an eternal glory that far outweighs them all"* (2 Corinthians 4.17).

It's as if Paul placed all the pain and persecution on one side of a scale and the promised eternal glory on the other and realized saying yes to Jesus was an easy decision. Like Moses, he looked beyond today to the reward from God he valued more than anything.

Which brings us back to Elisha. Without a word, Elijah walked up to him and threw his mantle around him. The mantle was the symbol of Elijah's prophetic authority. Tossing it on Elisha sent an obvious message, "I call on you to join me in my work as a prophet of God."

It took a nano-second for Elisha to count the cost and say yes. He would sacrifice friends and family. The fact he had 12 yoke of oxen indicated he possessed great wealth and a secure future, but he turned his back on it to follow Elijah.

Elisha destroyed the tools of his trade in a going away party. He slaughtered his oxen and lit a bonfire with his plowing equipment to cook the meat for his family and friends. This was more than a barbecue to bid farewell to loved ones. It signaled Elisha's total commitment to follow Elijah. With his oxen and plow burnt to a crisp, he had nothing to return to if he changed his mind down the road. He'd burned his bridges, and there was no turning back. Any temptation to return to his old life went up in a puff of smoke.

Elisha counted the cost and decided a yes to God was worth more than everything he had combined. Tens of millions of saints from Noah to the present day agree. What about you?

Kyle Idleman makes an important point. "The problem isn't that we need to choose to follow Jesus; the problem is that we have tried to follow him without leaving something behind" (*Gods at War*).

Idleman is right. Multitudes of Christians today are more like the rich young ruler who wouldn't part with his riches than they are like Matthew who *"got up, left everything and followed him"* (Luke 5.28). Two wealthy men. Same invitation from Jesus. One saw greater value in Jesus, one cherished his fortune more. One left all his money behind, the other wouldn't.

Seems clear which man made the right decision when you read Jesus' words: *"Do not store up for yourselves treasures on earth, where moth and rust destroy, and where thieves break in and steal. But store up for yourselves treasures in heaven, where moth and rust do not destroy, and where thieves do not break in and steal"* (Matthew 6.19-20).

What is more valuable — something temporary or something eternal?

Elisha had to weigh the value of following Elijah against family, wealth, and security. Moses had to assess if disgrace and eventual reward for the cause of Christ was of greater value than the treasures of Egypt that could have been his. Paul, Matthew, and the four fishermen had to evaluate if leaving everything behind was worth following Jesus.

You must as well. A non-decision is a decision — a decision to reject Jesus and God's call.

Factor in these words from Jesus as you choose: *"Everyone who has left houses or brothers or sisters or father or mother or wife or children or fields for my sake will receive a hundred times as much and will inherit eternal life"* (Matthew 19.29).

What you do next is up to you.

***Run with it*:**
The value of something is determined by how much someone will pay for it. How valuable is saying yes to Jesus to you?

DAY 23
The Final Straw

... because you have sold yourself to do evil in the eyes of the Lord, I am going to bring disaster on you.
(1 Kings 21.20-21)

Read 1 Kings 21.1-24

World War I began in 1914, but the United States didn't enter the war until 1917. The U.S. had a policy of neutrality and many of her citizens viewed the war as a dispute between "old world" powers that had nothing to do with them.

In January 1917, the British intercepted the Zimmerman Telegram, named after its sender Arthur Zimmerman, the German Foreign Secretary. In the secret telegram to the German ambassador in Mexico, Zimmerman proposed an alliance with Mexico against the United States. For their help, Germany promised them Texas, New Mexico, and Arizona after they won the war.

The Zimmerman Telegram turned out to be the final straw for President Woodrow Wilson and the U.S.

Congress. Neutrality was shelved and the U.S. declared war on Germany and its allies.

God has a breaking point too, a final straw which changes mercy into wrath. When a nation, family, or individual crosses the line one too many times, a just God must punish their rebellion and sin. Justice is one of God's qualities people often overlook. They view God as a tottering old grandfather who looks the other way when his grandchildren do something wrong because he can't bring himself to discipline them. But that's not God.

God is just, so he must punish sin. He can't ignore it or say it doesn't matter. He can't let sin pass with a shrug of his shoulders. If he did, he'd be neither holy nor just.

We have a strong sense of justice ourselves. We want to see the bad guy get what's coming to him. When a judge gives a criminal a slap on the wrist, we know justice wasn't served. After a repeat sex offender is out on bail days after his arrest and rapes another child, our blood boils because we know justice demands harsh sentences for such horrific crimes.

God is just. Wrongdoing must be punished. The wrath of God will be released on those who refuse to repent of what they've done and turn to God. Don't misunderstand — God doesn't have an itchy trigger finger. He isn't on a stakeout to catch your next sin so he can punish you. He is not your enemy. He loves you and he's made a way for you to avoid his wrath and justice — Jesus' death on the cross for you satisfies the justice of God. If you repeatedly snub his offer to absolve you of all your sin through faith in Jesus, justice is waiting for you in the wings.

Peter states, *"He is patient with you, not wanting anyone to perish, but everyone to come to repentance"* (2 Pet. 3.9). That's the heart of God. But anyone who declines to repent and turn to God triggers his justice and overrides his patience.

The final straw for Ahab came when he murdered Naboth and seized his land. They were neighbors, and the king decided he wanted Naboth's vineyard to plant a vegetable garden. Naboth said no, citing an ancient law prohibiting this kind of property transfer (see Numbers 36.7).

The king stomped home, crawled into bed, pulled the covers over his head, and pouted like a spoiled brat. Disgusted by his behavior, Jezebel ordered him to grow up and act like a king; she'd get the vineyard for him. She sent letters to the elders of Naboth's city, ordering them to set him up. Accuse him of cursing God and the king, and stone him to death for his offense. When the elders carried out her instructions and Naboth was dead, Ahab took possession of his vineyard.

It was the final straw. God sent word to Elijah to pronounce judgment on him. *"This is what the Lord says: 'Have you not murdered a man and seized his property?' Then say to him, 'This is what the Lord says: In the place where dogs licked up Naboth's blood, dogs will lick up your blood!'"* (1 Kings 21.19).

But God wasn't finished. Jezebel and all of Ahab's descendants fell under the wrath of God too — *"every last male"* descendant of Ahab would be killed (1 Kings 21.21), and *"dogs will devour Jezebel by the wall of Jezreel"* (1 Kings 21.23).

No one could accuse God of being unfair in passing sentence on Ahab, Jezebel, and his descendants. It was long overdue. For 24 years, Elijah confronted Ahab for his sinful behavior and proved to him the Lord God was God, not Baal. But Ahab stubbornly refused to abolish Baal worship in Israel and give his devotion to the one true God, the God of Elijah.

Once someone crosses a line known only to God, justice kicks in. Ahab crossed the line when he eliminated God from his life for good. It was too late for him now. The die had been cast and judgment day arrived.

The sentence against Ahab may seem like overkill with all the blood and guts and gore, but a day is coming that will make Ahab's punishment look like a cut on your finger.

"Then the kings of the earth, the princes, the generals, the rich, the mighty, and every slave and every free man hid in caves and among the rocks of the mountains. They called to the mountains and the rocks, 'Fall on us and hide us from the face of him who sits on the throne and from the wrath of the Lamb! For the great day of their wrath has come, and who can stand?'" (Revelation 16.15-17).

After that terrible day, an eternal sentence to hell without parole or a lighter sentence for good behavior arrives. Hell is real, and its description in Scripture is horrid. But the day of the Lord's wrath and hell are avoidable. *"Repent then and turn to God so that your sins may be wiped out, that times of refreshing may come from the Lord"* (Romans 3.19).

Run with it:

"Justice is not something God has. Justice is something that God is" (A.W. Tozer).

DAY 24

Merciful God

"Have you noticed how Ahab has humbled himself before me? Because he has humbled himself, I will not bring this disaster in his day."
(1 Kings 21.29)

Read 1 Kings 21.17-19, 27-29

A mother approached Napoleon seeking a pardon for her son. The emperor gruffly replied that the young man had committed an offense twice and justice demanded death.

"I don't ask for justice," the mother explained. "I plead for mercy."

"Your son doesn't deserve mercy," Napoleon stated.

"Sir," the woman cried, "it wouldn't be mercy if he deserved it."

Mercy and justice are opposites. Justice means sin and disobedience must be punished. The key word in that sentence is "must." Justice doesn't leave any other options. If God turned a blind eye to sin and let people get away with it without consequences, he would not be just.

God is also *"rich in mercy"* (Ephesians 2.4). Mercy means you don't get what you deserve. You deserve a lifetime of misery, suffering, sadness, God's wrath, and hell.

Because God is merciful, he doesn't want to punish us, but because he's just, he must. What a quandary, but he had a solution — Jesus. Sin must be punished, so he sent his Son to die in our place to pay the penalty we earned. With justice satisfied through Jesus, God can offer mercy

Ahab deserved the judgment God pronounced against him. Look at the case against him: he *"did more to provoke the Lord, the God of Israel, to anger than did all the kings of Israel before him"* (1 Kings 16.33). He promoted Baal worship and banned the worship of God in Israel. He murdered Naboth and stole his vineyard. For his behavior, he, Jezebel, and all his descendants were sentenced to die. The moment for God's justice had arrived.

"When Ahab heard these words, he tore his clothes, put on sackcloth and fasted. He lay in sackcloth and went about meekly" (1 Kings 21.27). Throughout Old Testament days, these were the signs of mourning and repentance. Ahab finally saw the light and regretted his lifetime of rebellion against God. Or did he?

In 2 Corinthians 7.8-11, Paul reveals there are two kinds of sorrow over sin — worldly sorrow and godly sorrow.

- Worldly sorrow is when you're sorry you got *caught* for doing something wrong, and sorry you'll suffer *consequences* for it. Paul said it leads to death because it doesn't result in a change of direction.
- Godly sorrow is when you're sorry for doing something wrong. Paul states it *"brings repentance that leads to salvation and leaves no regret."* It's when the fact you sinned disturbs you.

Worldly sorrow vows to be more careful next time so you don't get caught. Godly sorry vows to never do it again even if you can devise a foolproof plan so you don't get caught next time.

According to Bible commentator Matthew Poole, Ahab fell into the worldly sorrow column. "This humiliation or repentance of Ahab's was only external and superficial, arising from the terror of God's judgments; and not sincere and serious, proceeding from the love of God, or a true sense of his sin, or a solemn purpose of amendment of his life, as appears, because all the particulars of his repentance here, are external and ritual only; nor is there the least intimation of any one sign or fruit of his true repentance, as that he restored Naboth's land, or reproved his infamous wife; but in the very next chapter you find him returning to his former vomit."

Yet God responds to Ahab with mercy: *"Have you noticed how Ahab has humbled himself before me?"* (1

Kings 21.29). Did Ahab fool God by his pretend repentance? Of course not. No one fools God. Rather, God's reaction tells us something amazing about him — he favors mercy over judgment. It doesn't matter the sin; he longs to forgive and shower us with mercy and grace. Even the slightest step toward repentance (like Ahab's) ignites God's mercy.

The book of Jeremiah indicts Judah of such sin, God told Jeremiah not to pray to reverse God's intended judgment on them. Nothing would change his mind; the Judge had handed down their sentence.

Yet later in his prophecy, Jeremiah recorded God's promise: *"In those days, at that time, declares the Lord, search will be made for Israel's guilt, but there will be none, and for the sins of Judah, but none will be found, for I will forgive the remnant I spare"* (Jeremiah 50.20). Insert your name for "Israel's" and "Judah" and marvel at the mercy of God for you.

If a prosecuting attorney (Satan) wanted to find evidence to present against you before the Judge of the universe, he would come to court empty-handed. No case to present because there's no evidence of a single wrong.

When God saw Ahab's repentance — superficial though it was — he delayed judgment. He offered Ahab extra time to genuinely change his ways. God delayed the sentence he imposed upon Ahab and his entire family, but he did not revoke it. God vowed to mete out judgment after Ahab died.

When anyone turns from their sin and turns to Jesus, *"mercy triumphs over judgment"* (James 2.13). That's always what God prefers.

Run with it:

Contemplate your sorrow over your sin — are you sorry because you got caught and now must pay the penalty, or are you sorry you sinned? Does your sorrow lead you to changes in your life, or does it lead you to be more careful so you don't get caught next time?

DAY 25
Your Verse

There was never a man like Ahab who sold himself to do evil in the eyes of the Lord.
(1 Kings 21.25)

Read 1 Kings 21.25-26

One morning in 1888, Alfred Nobel scanned the local newspaper and read a story that alarmed him so badly he dropped the paper — his own obituary!

The obituary resulted from a simple journalistic error. Alfred's brother had died, and the reporter attributed the death to the wrong brother. It would disturb anyone under those circumstances, but to Alfred, the shock was overwhelming. For the first time in his life he saw himself as the world saw him.

In the public's eye, Nobel's entire purpose in life was to enjoy the immense fortune he made from his invention of dynamite. They recognized none of his true intentions to break down barriers to achieve peace. He was a merchant of death, and that is what they would remember him for.

What if you woke up one day to read your obituary in the newspaper or online and viewed yourself through the eyes of your family and friends? A revelation of how your neighbors and those you work with and go to church with you view you? Two hundred words that sum up your life.

Have you considered what your obituary will say about you? Ahab didn't, and worse still, he didn't have a reporter from the Jezreel Journal write it. God, who saw everything he did, said, thought, and tried to hide, authored his obituary. Two verses of Scripture. Forty-four words.

"There was never a man like Ahab, who sold himself to do evil in the eyes of the Lord, urged on by Jezebel his wife. He behaved in the vilest manner by going after idols, like the Amorites the Lord drove out before Israel" (1 Kings 21.25-26).

That's a tough assessment of a life. Harsh, but accurate. How would God recap your life in one or two verses? What would you like God to write?

Maybe something like he wrote of David — *"I have found David son of Jesse, a man after my own heart; he will do everything I want him to do"* (Acts 13.22).

Or Stephen — *"A man full of faith and the Holy Spirit"* (Acts 6.5).

Perhaps Noah — *"Noah did everything just as God commanded him"* (Genesis 6.22).

King Josiah would be a good choice — *"Neither before nor after Josiah was there a king like him who turned to the Lord as he did — with all his heart and with all his soul and with all his strength"* (2 Kings 23.25).

Perhaps this snapshot of Peter when Jesus asked him to let down his nets for a catch — "*Master, we've worked hard all night and haven't caught anything,* but because you say so, *I will let down the nets*" (Luke 5.5).

Far more important than what the people around you see is what God sees when he records your actions and words and, most notably, your heart.

God will capture the story of your life. It will be unique to you, not a duplicate of anyone else. It will be accurate and true. No fluff piece with exaggerated praise and failures whitewashed from your verse.

As Alfred Nobel read the obituary of "his death" with horror and learned what people thought of him, he resolved to change their perception of him. In his last will and testament, he ordered the administrator to disperse his vast wealth with annual awards to individuals who made outstanding contributions in physics, chemistry, physiology or medicine, literature, and peace.

Today when people hear the name Alfred Nobel, they think "Nobel Peace Prize," not "inventor of dynamite." He intentionally changed people's perception of him rather than leave it to chance.

What will you do on purpose so God could write a verse about your life you'd be happy for others to read?

You will leave a legacy when you're gone. It will be what others remember you for. What was important to you. What you valued. What your relationship with God was like.

As you get older, you will evaluate your life and your choices. Did I make a positive difference in the lives of those I loved? Did my life have purpose? What will people remember me for? Did my life matter? Will anyone miss me? Will it be hard to replace me? Did I love well? Was Jesus at the center of my life and did I represent him well?

God's opinion about these questions is the only one that counts. You can fool others and bask in the praise of men, but what matters in the end is the verse God writes about you.

Imagine God boasting about you to Satan like this: *"Have you considered my servant,* (insert your name here)? *There is no one on earth like him; he is blameless and upright, a man who fears God and shuns evil"* (Job 1.8).

Imagine how a legacy like that would influence those you love. How much positive impact it would have on the kingdom. Your verse can inspire others. Let God have full rein to do in you and through you whatever he wants.

O, what a verse he'll write!

Run with it:

Take a few minutes and think through three questions. [1] If God wrote a verse to summarize my life, what would he write? [2] What do I want him to write?

[3] What is one thing I will begin today so God writes that about me?

DAY 26
Practical Atheists

"Is it because there is no God in Israel that you are going off to consult Baal-zebub, the god of Ekron?
(2 Kings 1.3)

Read 2 Kings 1.1-18

An atheist walked through the woods, admiring all the "accidents" that evolution had created. The trees, the rivers, the animals. As he walked beside the river, he heard a rustling in the bushes behind him. He turned and saw a seven-foot grizzly bear charging towards him.

He sprinted off as fast as possible up the path. Glancing over his shoulder, he saw the grizzly closing the space between them. Somehow, he willed himself to go even faster. He peeked behind him again, and the bear was right on his heels. In a last ditch attempt to get away, he dodged to his right, but tripped over a branch laying on the path. Before he could get up, the bear stood over him, reaching for him with its left paw and raising its right paw to strike him.

In a desperate panic, the atheist cried, "Oh God, help!" Time stopped. The bear froze. The forest was silent. Even the river stopped moving. A bright light shone upon the man, and he heard a voice from out of the sky. "You deny my existence for all these years, teach others I don't exist, and even credit creation to a cosmic accident. Do you expect me to help you out of this predicament? Do you want to become a believer now?"

The atheist stared into the light and said, "I would feel like a hypocrite to become a Christian after all these years, but perhaps you could make the bear a Christian?"

"Okay," said the voice.

The light went out and everything returned to normal except the bear. It brought both paws together, bowed its head, and said: "Lord, for this food which I am about to receive, I am truly thankful."

Have you heard of a practical atheist? Let Charles Spurgeon explain, "Let me ask you, how many atheists are now in this house [church]? Perhaps not a single one of you would accept the title, and yet, if you live Monday morning to Saturday night in the same way as you would if there were no God, you are practical atheists."

Craig Groeschel calls them Christian atheists and defines them as people who believe in God but live as if God didn't exist. They cope with all the pressure and stress of home and work on their own, only rarely turning to the God they profess is all they need.

King Ahaziah was a practical atheist. Ahaziah was the eldest son of Ahab who assumed the throne after Ahab died. Like father, like son, Ahaziah served and worshiped Baal, provoking God to anger. In the second year of his reign, he fell and seriously injured himself. He sent messengers to Baal-zebub, the god of Ekron — not the God of Israel — to ask if he would recover.

God dispatched an angel to Elijah with a message to relay to the king. It's a piercing question every Christian should ponder because it sets apart a genuine Christian from a practical atheist. *"This is what the Lord says: Is it because there is no God in Israel that you are going off to consult Baal-zebub, the god of Ekron?"* (2 Kings 1.6). God says Ahaziah's decision to turn to a false god shouted loud and clear he didn't think the Lord God could help him.

What about you? You say you believe God is your refuge and strength, an ever-present help in times of trouble (Psalm 46.1). But if your first move when you're in trouble is anywhere but God, do you really believe what you claim? Aren't you living like a practical atheist?

"Let's say it's been a terrible day at the office. You come home and go — where? To the refrigerator for comfort food like ice cream? To the phone to vent with your most trusted friend? Do you seek escape in novels or movies or video games or pornography? Where do you look for emotional rescue?" (Kyle Idleman)

Take a moment for self-examination:

Where do you go when you are weary and need rest?

Where do you turn when fear overcomes you?

Where do you go when your hopes are dashed?

Where do you turn when you're hurting?
Where do you go to relieve stress and pressure?
Where do you turn when you get news your daughter has cancer?
Where do you go when your heart is broken?
Where do you turn when you don't know what to do?

Christians run to Jesus as their first resort in every difficulty they encounter and every decision they must make. Practical atheists don't.

Christians go to Jesus to find rest when they are weary and burdened (Matthew 11.28). Practical atheists don't.

Christians put their hope in the Lord and he renews their strength (Isaiah 40.31). Practical atheists don't.

Christians come to Jesus, the bread of life and spring of living water, when they are hungry and thirsty and find he satisfies the deepest longings of their soul (John 6.35, 4.10). Practical atheists don't.

To paraphrase Isaiah 55.2, why spend your time, money, and energy on what does not satisfy?

The solution is simple. Stop running from God; turn around and run toward him as your first resort whenever you're in need.

Run with it:

If you scanned the self-examination above, go back and take an honest look at yourself. Do you live as a Christian or as a practical atheist?

DAY 27
Escape Clause

Elijah said to Elisha, "Stay here; the Lord has sent me to Bethel." But Elisha said, "As surely as the Lord lives and you live, I will not leave you."
(2 Kings 2.2)

Read 2 Kings 2.1-13

In 2006, the third installment of *The Santa Clause* movies came out. Starring Tim Allen and Martin Short, it was called *The Escape Clause*. Scott Calvin (Allen) took the mantle of Santa Claus 12 years earlier in the first movie, but trouble was brewing.

The Council of Legendary Figures: Mother Nature, Father Time, the Easter Bunny, Cupid, the Tooth Fairy, and the Sandman, called a meeting to come up with a solution to the bad behavior of Jack Frost (Short). He'd been causing trouble because he didn't have a holiday or special occasion in his honor. The Council sentenced him to community service at the North Pole.

But Jack Frost launched a plot to trick Santa into exercising the "Santa clause." If invoked by saying, "I wish I had never been Santa at all," Scott Calvin's tenure as Santa would end. Frost tricked Calvin into repeating the phrase and became Santa himself. The rest of the movie shows how Calvin tried to get Frost to use the Santa clause himself and retake his role as Santa Claus.

An escape clause is part of a contract specifying conditions which frees one party from his obligation spelled out in the contract. He can "escape" his legal responsibility by exercising the clause.

In 2 Kings 2, Elijah gives Elisha an opportunity to exercise the escape clause in his commitment to succeed him in his prophetic ministry. Elisha had previously gone all in as Elijah's replacement. He left everything to follow him (1 Kings 19.19-21). Now with Elijah's departure to heaven nearing, he needed to ascertain Elisha's continued commitment to his earlier decision.

Enough time had passed for Elisha to see with his own eyes the hardship and opposition Elijah had to endur as God's prophet. As before, he must weigh the costs vs. the benefits. It didn't take him long to decide saying yes to God had far greater value than throwing in the towel, despite the certain adversity awaiting him.

Elijah paid a final visit to the schools of the prophets in Gilgal, Bethel, and Jericho on his way to the spot where God would take him to heaven. At each town as he prepared to go on to the next one, he told Elisha, *"Stay here."* But each time, Elisha passed the loyalty test and answered, *"As surely as the Lord lives and you live, I will not leave you"* (2 Kings 2.2,4,6).

The duo crossed the Jordan River and mid-chat, God whisked Elijah to heaven in a whirlwind. Elijah left his mantle at Elisha's feet. It didn't fall from heaven and rest on his shoulders. Once again, Elisha had to choose — pick up the mantle and follow in Elijah's footsteps, or let it lie and go home.

The door stood wide open for Elisha to walk away if he considered the cost too great. Instead, he slammed the door shut, locked it, threw away the key, and picked up the mantle.

Jesus always left the door open for his followers to rethink their pledge to him. In the final year of his ministry, Jesus raised the bar for the multitudes who came to see him dazzle them with miracles and fill their bellies with free food.

The day after he fed over 5000 people, Jesus demanded a commitment from them. He wouldn't be their meal train any longer; he must be their Lord, the Bread of Life, who gives eternal life to all who believe in him. The multitudes considered the requirement too much to ask of them. *"From this time many of his disciples turned back and no longer followed him"* (John 6.66).

Jesus did two surprising things next. First, he refused to lower the bar to persuade the crowds to stay. Though it broke his heart, he… let… them… go.

Second, Jesus pivots to the Twelve, *"You do not want to leave too, do you?"* (John 6.67). Three years earlier, each of these men left everything to follow him. Now, as opposition to Jesus replaces popularity, he offers them an escape clause. They can go if they want.

Without hesitation, Peter spoke for the Twelve. *"Lord, to whom shall we go? You have the words of eternal life"* (John 6.68). He quickly reviewed what his life was like before he met Jesus and what it's been like since. Peter concluded it was an easy decision — Jesus today, tomorrow, and for the rest of his life.

Personalize Ruth's unwavering commitment to Naomi and turn it into your pledge to Jesus.

Orpah kissed her mother-in-law goodbye, but Ruth clung to her. "Look," Naomi said, "your sister-in-law is going back to her people and her gods. Go back with her." But Ruth replied, "Don't urge me to leave you or turn back from you. Where you go I will go, where you stay I will stay. Your people will be my people and your God my God. Where you die I will die, and there I will be buried. May the Lord deal with me, be it ever so severely, if anything but death separates you and me" (Ruth 1.16-17).

***Run with it*:**

Grab a pen and paper. Draw a diagonal line down the center and list the benefits you've experienced and have been promised on one side, and the losses you've suffered and expect on the other. The next time you wonder whether it's worth it to follow Jesus, read your lists. Then decide.

DAY 28

What Can I Do For You?

Elijah said to Elisha, "Tell me, what can I do for you before I am taken?" "Let me inherit a double portion of your spirit," Elisha replied.
(2 Kings 2.9)

Read 2 Kings 2.9-15

A despondent woman spied a bottle on the sand as she walked along the beach. Curious, she picked up the bottle and pulled out the cork. Whoosh! A big puff of smoke appeared.

"You have released me from my prison," the genie told her. "I grant you three wishes. But take care because every wish I grant you your husband will get double."

"That doesn't seem right," the woman said. "That bum left me for another woman."

She shrugged her shoulders, thought for a minute, and asked for a million dollars. There was a flash of light, and a million dollars appeared at her feet. At the same instant, her wayward husband found twice that amount of cash on his kitchen table.

"And your second wish?"

"Genie, I want the world's most expensive diamond necklace." Another flash of light, and the woman was holding the precious treasure. Meanwhile, her husband searched the internet for a gem broker to buy his latest bonanza.

"Genie, is it true my husband gets double of anything I wish for next?"

"Yes, it's true."

"You're sure?" The genie nodded his head.

"Then I'm ready for my last wish," the woman said. "Scare me half to death."

On the day of his trip Home, Elijah used his mantle to divide the waters of the Jordan River so he and Elisha could cross over on dry ground. Once on the other side, Elijah turned to Elisha and said, *"Tell me, what can I do for you before I am taken from you?"* (2 Kings 2.9). Given a blank slate to ask for anything at all, Elisha answered, *"Let me inherit a double portion of your spirit"* (2 Kings 2.9).

At first glance, it may appear arrogant of Elisha to ask a double portion of Elijah's spirit, but his request had nothing to do with fame and greatness. According to Jewish law, the firstborn son received a double portion of his father's inheritance when he died (see Deuteronomy 21.17). Elisha wished to be regarded as Elijah's firstborn son in ministry. He yearned for the spiritual power of Elijah to carry out the prophetic ministry entrusted to him.

The pair walked and talked together for a while (wonder what they talked about) until God sent fiery horses and a chariot to escort Elijah to heaven. After the awe of the moment wore off, Elisha picked up Elijah's mantle and walked back to the bank of the Jordan River. He struck the water with it and watched it divide just as it had earlier that day when Elijah hit it with his mantle.

The company of the prophets from Jericho saw the miracle and recognized *"the spirit of Elijah is resting on Elisha"* (2 Kings 2.15). The transfer of authority and power to Elisha as God's prophet was complete. Elisha performed more miracles than any other prophet in the Old Testament and fearlessly delivered God's message to kings and citizens alike.

What if Jesus approached you this afternoon and said, "Tell me, what can I do for you?" What would you say to him? Don't rush on to the next paragraph. Formulate your answer.

There isn't data to indicate Jesus asked the apostles that question, but he wanted them to have something more powerful than a double portion of Elijah's spirit. He gave them Holy Spirit.

"You will receive power when the Holy Spirit comes on you; and you will be my witnesses..." (Acts 1.8). This was the same helper Jesus promised in the last days before his crucifixion in John 14 and 16. Holy Spirit is Jesus in a different form who would be with them and in them forever. He would remind them of the things Jesus had spoken and lead them into truth. Through them, the

Spirit would convict the world of sin, righteousness, and judgment. With their cooperation, he would transform them from the inside out.

When they received Holy Spirit in Acts 2, he put God's words in their mouths. After Jesus' crucifixion, they hid in fear and silence from the Jewish authorities. After they were indwelt with God's Spirit, they boldly shared the gospel in the presence of those who killed Jesus and could do the same to them.

This wasn't an isolated event either. The Spirit of Jesus provided the pivotal spark in the transformation of their entire lives. Courage, confidence, and Christlike character. Power to do miracles, heal the sick, and set captives free from decades of demonic oppression and unyielding strongholds. Bitterness, prejudice, and legalism flushed from their hearts.

Only the Spirit's presence could fashion such an amazing makeover. "Without the Spirit of God, we can do nothing. We are as ships without wind. We are useless" (Charles Spurgeon). We are like floor lamps disconnected from the electrical outlet — powerless and unable to change.

But power is readily available to every Christian. You don't have to do anything special to entice the Spirit of God to live inside you. He's already in there. You just need to raise your sails to catch the wind of the Spirit who will lead you in the ways of God. You must stay plugged in to him so he is free to do in you and through you whatever he wants.

***Run with it*:**
If Jesus asked you today what he can do for you, what would you say?

DAY 29

Homecoming

As they were walking along and talking together, suddenly a chariot of fire and horses of fire appeared and separated the two of them, and Elijah went up to heaven in a whirlwind.
(2 Kings 2.11)

Read 2 Kings 2.11-12

A woman had terminal cancer and was given three months to live. As she began to get her things in order, she called her pastor and asked him to come to her house to discuss some of her last wishes.

She told him the songs she wanted sung at her funeral service, what Scripture verses she would like read, and what outfit she wanted to be buried in. She requested him to place her favorite Bible in the casket with her.

After a few consoling words and prayer for her, the pastor stood to leave. The woman grabbed his arm and said, "Wait. There's one more thing, pastor."

"What's that?" asked the pastor.

"This is important," she said. "I want to be buried with a fork in my right hand."

The pastor stared at the woman with a puzzled look on his face, not knowing what to say.

The woman explained. "In all my years attending church socials and potluck dinners, when they cleared the dishes of the main course, someone would always say, 'Keep your fork.' I knew something better was coming — dessert, something like velvety chocolate cake or deep-dish apple pie.

"So, when people see me in my casket with a fork in my hand and they ask, 'What's with the fork?' I want you to tell them: 'Keep your fork. The best is yet to come!'"

It really is, you know. Heaven awaits. The Great Homecoming. The "and they lived happily ever after" ending to the story of your life. The best day of your life here will seem like a train wreck there.

How could it not be the best day ever?

"[God] will wipe every tear from [your] eyes. There will be no more death or mourning or crying or pain" (Revelation 21.4). That's what I can expect in heaven? Count me in!

Everything you've sacrificed for Jesus will be more than rewarded. *"Everyone who has left houses or brothers or sisters or father or mother or wife or children or fields for my sake will receive a hundred times as much and will inherit eternal life"* (Matthew 19.29).

Heaven is a place where you'll see Jesus and hang out with him forever. No wonder you'll rejoice and leap for joy (Luke 6.23). It'll be that good — better than you can even imagine. *

The promise of heaven stirred believers from Abraham to the present to not lose heart when everything went against them. It's what motivated them to stay faithful to God and not be seduced by the short-term pleasures and empty promises this world offered them. And you.

John Burke said, "We are told by the apostle Paul to imagine Heaven — to set our minds on the realities of Heaven, so that it changes how we live today." [Here are a few verses that support Burke's statement that would be worthwhile to read and ponder: Colossian 3.1-4; Romans 8.18; 2 Corinthians 4.18-21; Hebrews 11.24-26, 32-40; 2 Timothy 4.7-8; 2 Peter 3.13-14.]

The writer of Hebrews relates how the hope of heaven weighted every decision in favor of choosing God regardless of whatever else was proposed as a better deal.

"All these people were still living by faith when they died. They did not receive the things promised; they only saw them and welcomed them from a distance, admitting they were foreigners and strangers on earth. People who say such things show that they are looking for a country of their own. If they had been thinking of the country they had left, they would have had opportunity to return. Instead, they were longing for a better country — a heavenly one. Therefore God is not ashamed to be called their God, for he has prepared a city for them" (Hebrews 11.13-16).

Heaven's greater value motivated Elijah to remain faithful to God in the face of persecution, death threats, disappointment, fear, depression, loneliness, and opposition. If he hadn't fixed his eyes on heaven, he would have quit long before God sent fiery horses and a chariot to carry him to heaven.

Max Lucado wrote, "God never said that the journey would be easy, but He did say that the arrival would be worthwhile."

Like Moses in Egypt, Elijah regarded mistreatment and disgrace as far greater value than making nice with Ahab and Jezebel because he looked ahead to his reward. Jesus welcomed him with a bear hug and a huge smile on his face, "Well done Elijah, my good and faithful servant... Come and share my happiness" (Matthew 25.21). In that moment, Elijah counted all the suffering he had endured worth it. His afflictions didn't compare to the glory of gazing into Jesus' eyes and hearing those words.

That welcome awaits you too, my friend. Let heaven inspire you to fight the good fight, finish your race strong, and stay faithful until your last breath. Let it convince you not to settle for second best, the only thing the world can offer. Don't quit. Don't look back. Fix your mind on what your Homecoming will be like.

Borrow Paul's viewpoint: *I press on toward the goal to win the prize for which God has called me heavenward in Christ Jesus* (Philippians 3.14).

***Run with it*:**
According to Billy Graham, "God will prepare everything for our perfect happiness in heaven, and if it takes my dog being there, I believe he'll be there."

DAY 30
Elijahs of God

"Where now is the Lord, the God of Elijah?"
(2 Kings 2.14)

Read 2 Kings 2.11-15

The Japanese eat very little fat and suffer fewer heart attacks than Brits or Americans. The French eat lots of fat and still suffer fewer heart attacks than Brits or Americans.

The Japanese don't drink much red wine and have fewer heart attacks than Brits and Americans. Italians drink excessive amounts of red wine and have fewer heart attacks than Brits or Americans.

What's the conclusion? Eat and drink whatever you want. It's speaking English that kills you.

Faulty conclusions are easy to make. One that hinders Christians today from seeing God do the sort of things he did through the saints we read about in the Bible is that we believe they were a cut above us. We'll never be like them or do what they did because they were special and we're ordinary.

Perhaps this faulty reasoning explains why Elisha took Elijah's mantle to the Jordan River and struck the water with it. Elijah was a hard act to follow, and Elisha wondered if he could do what Elijah had done.

Mere moments before God took Elijah to heaven, he parted the waters of the Jordan River with his mantle and he and Elisha crossed over on dry ground (2 Kings 2.7-8). Two other heroes of the faith did the same before them — Moses at the Red Sea (Exodus 14.5-22) and Joshua at this very river (Joshua 3.14-17). For Elisha to think anyone would mention him in the same breath with Moses, Joshua, and Elijah was more than he could imagine. They were superstars.

Only one way to find out. Elisha picked up Elijah's mantle and walked to the banks of the Jordan. *"Where now is the Lord, the God of Elijah?"* He struck the water with the mantle and God answered immediately — *"it divided to the right and to the left"* (2 Kings 2.14).

God confirmed in that moment, not only for Elisha but also for you, that his presence is multi-generational. His presence linked Elisha with Elijah, who linked Elijah with Joshua, who linked Joshua with Moses. God's presence and power passes from one generation to the next... all the way to yours!

People come and people go, but God comes and stays. He is right here, right now, making accessible to you everything he made available to those you read about in the Bible. He is the same yesterday, today, and forever.

God hasn't gone anywhere, and he's not going anywhere. What he did before, he will do again.

Dr. Warren W. Wiersbe wrote, "Some may ask, 'Where is the Lord God of Elijah?' (2 Kings 2:14). Perhaps the better question is, where are the Elijahs?" Likewise, Leonard Ravenhill noted, "To the question, 'Where is the Lord God of Elijah?' (2 Kings 2:14) we answer, 'Where He has always been — on the throne!' But where are the Elijahs of God?'"

Where *are* the Elijahs of God in the twenty-first century?

Christians who pray and obey.

Believers passionate about revival in their nation.

Christ-followers who don't let fear, intimidation, or persecution stop them from doing anything God calls them to do.

Men and women of God who trust him with so much confidence they climb out on a limb and put him on the spot so he can prove to sceptics and non-believers he alone is God.

Our mistake is to believe we could never do what the men and women in the Bible did because we aren't as good as them. This erroneous conclusion is rooted in a comparison between today's believers and the believers we read about in God's Word. But that's a flawed assessment because the focus should be on the unchanging God who worked these mighty deeds through these people.

It wasn't the power, godliness, or talents of Elijah, Elisha, Joshua, Moses, or any other of the greats in the Bible that parted waters, raised the dead, brought water out of rocks, caused the walls of Jericho to cave in, killed giants, survived a fiery furnace, shut the mouths of lions, or defeated armies over ten times the size of their own. Their greatness stemmed from God's greatness, their power from God's power. What God did before, he will do again if we'll let him.

The power of God did each of these mighty deeds through ordinary men and women who trusted him and believed nothing was impossible for him. The God who did all the feats you read about through believers in Scripture extends his supernatural power to you today.

"Do not we rest in our day too much on the arm of flesh? Cannot the same wonders be done now as of old? Do not the eyes of the Lord still run to and fro throughout the whole earth to show Himself strong on behalf of those who put their trust in Him? [2 Chronicles 16.9] Oh, that God would give me more practical faith in Him! Where is now the Lord God of Elijah? He is waiting for Elijah to call on Him." (James Gilmour).

Call on him, my friend, and watch in amazement as he does in you and through you what he's always done.

Run with it:

"The need of the hour is for any army of soldiers dedicated to Jesus Christ, who believe that he is God, that he can fulfill every promise he ever made, and that nothing is too hard for him" (Dawson Trotman). Will you be that believer?

Thank you for reading this devotional based on the life of the prophet Elijah. I pray his example of unwavering faith and determined resolve encouraged you as you take your next steps on your spiritual journey. If it did, I'd love it if you would take a moment and write a review on Amazon and your other favorite book retailers. Tell your friends. Post something about how it inspired you on Facebook. Email friends and tell them how it helped you. Your recommendation through these ways could be the nudge a fellow believer needs to pick up this book and find the encouragement you found to persuade them to take their next step of faith.

Thank you! – SW

About Steve

Steve's lifelong passion has been to encourage and inspire Christ-followers on their long and sometimes treacherous spiritual journey Home. Over the years, he's learned valuable lessons from his own journey of faith and developed indispensable relationships that kept him from giving up when discouragement and doubts enveloped him. His purpose for the remaining years of his life is to share what he's learned in his everyday walk with God and in his study of the Word of God.

Steve married his college sweetheart, Becki, in 1974. She was an indispensable partner during their years together when Steve pastored five churches from 1976 to 2016. They have four grown children and eight grandchildren. From 1992 until 2017, Steve worked as a mail carrier for the United States Postal Service while also pastoring a church in Edgerton, Ohio, where he and his wife still live. Though retired from his bi-vocational jobs, he continues to engage with others to help them love Jesus and follow him their whole life long.

Always with an itch for writing to spur spiritual growth, Steve now writes novels, spiritual growth books, and devotionals (you can peruse his books in the pages that follow). He also writes a weekly column for two local newspapers called "*Pastor's Ponderings.*"

In his spare time, Steve enjoys reading, gardening, and landscaping around his house and as a free service for anyone who needs his expertise and labor. He stays connected with his Band of Brothers small group as they live out Ecclesiastes 4.9-12, Hebrews 10.24-25, and Acts 2.42 together.

Other Books by Steve

Cornered in Shallow Water: One Man's Journey from Crippling Fear to Faith and Freedom

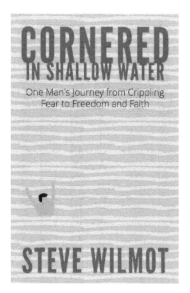

Gabriel Williams was dying inside. Little by little passion drained from him. Drip, drip, drip. Then a steady stream. Feeling no purpose. Going through the motions. Trancelike. Discouraged and stagnant.

He knew what he needed to do, but that was the problem. It scared him. The risks of taking this step were almost more than he could handle. He liked the comfort zone. And hated it at the same time.

He couldn't let his fear of taking this next step on his faith journey be one more item on his list of life regrets. But could he muster the courage to take the leap?

In "Cornered in Shallow Water," recipient of a Readers' Favorite 5-star review, Gabriel's story will show you how to face your fears and come out on the other side with greater faith, freedom and fulfillment.

This book is for you if you...

- Want to break the crippling grip of fear that prevents you from doing what you know God wants you to do
- Want to look back at the end of your life with fewer regrets
- Are no longer content to settle for the monotonous routine of daily life
- Aspire to step out of your comfort zone even though it scares you
- Are ready to dive into deep waters where you can't touch bottom
- Need encouragement to take risks in your faith journey

"Highly recommended! I simply couldn't put it down. Packed full of raw emotions, truth, wisdom, humor, love & victory! This book was written in such a relatable fashion with so many lessons built in. I have already bought a few books to share & I am certain I will be reading this over & over again! Great job!" [Reviewed by Codi]

Available on Amazon. E-Book
→ *www.amazon.com/dp/B086QHT3R7*

Paperback
→ *www.amazon.com/dp/B086PNZBCK*

Do It Scared: 20 Devotional Readings to Turn Scaredy-Cats into Warriors

The transformation from scaredy-cat to warrior is a process of increasing trust in God. Confidence that God is Who He says He is, and that He will do what He's said He will do. It's an ever-increasing awareness that God is with you, so you need not allow fear to control you.

Courage is not the absence of fear. It's a decision to do what you must do even though you're terrified. If you wait until you overcome your dread, you will never do anything meaningful. Sometimes, you just have to trust God and do it scared.

This little volume of 20 devotional readings will help set you free from being a scaredy-cat who stays in the safety of the boat when Jesus calls you to walk on water. They will make it easier for you to take risks you know God wants you to take. They will teach you that you can step out of your comfort zone and do daring exploits.

They won't eliminate fear from your life, but they will nudge you to live like the warrior God created you to be. They will provide the encouragement to do what God wants you to do even if you must do it scared.

"I am grateful to have stumbled upon this inspiring, encouraging book. I highly recommended it!" [Review from KA]

"I greatly enjoyed using this as my morning devotional. I have highlighted the text used in my Bible as a reminder of the thoughts the author brought out." [Reviewed by Pam]

Available on Amazon. E-Book
→ *www.amazon.com/B08GR8SP96*

Paperback
→ *www.amazon.com/B08HTM7ZMW*

Best of Pastor's Ponderings: 40 Reflections for Your Spiritual Journey

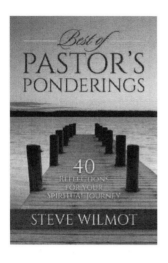

"Every saint has a past, and every sinner has a future.

"Every person God ever used had a past he or she was ashamed of, but that didn't matter to God. It didn't tie his hands. Just because you have a dark past doesn't mean God will toss you into the garbage heap as worthless. Far from it. Every saint has a past that Jesus Christ changed.

"But it's equally true that every sinner has a future. Look at Apostle Paul, for example."

We all need reminders and the lines above are a sample of those you'll find in this book. It's tough to trek the path of your spiritual journey. If you try to do it alone, it's near impossible.

This book will be a valuable companion through the difficulties and trials, victories and defeats, gains and losses Christians encounter on their pilgrimage toward Home.

These four-minute readings encourage Christ-followers to remember what really matters, to count on God's presence and promises more, and to deal with their regrets and move on. To hold on to hope even after a painful past tries to snuff it out and present-day struggles attempt to sink it. They call us to see life from God's perspective and to convince us that every hardship along the way will be worth it someday. Keep going and don't give up.

"I am part way through the book. Each "pondering" is easily readable, relatable, and relevant. If you are not the type to sit down and read long chapters at a time but still want a great and insightful spiritual book, this is it!" [Review from Amazon Customer]

"This is an excellent devotional book. The devotions don't take long to read but are filled with uplifting words that will have you thinking on them throughout the day." [Reviewed by Mike]

Available on Amazon. E-Book
→ *www.amazon.com/dp/B08XR1BSF1*

Paperback
→ *www.amazon.com/dp/B08X2FFBN1*

30 Days with Joshua: Inspiration from Joshua's Spiritual Journey for Yours (A Devotional)

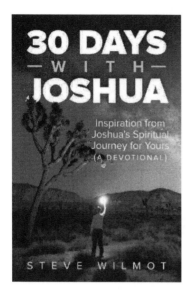

30 Days with Joshua is the first in a series of devotionals designed to focus on one Bible character at a time where you can glean guidelines for your spiritual journey. Joshua's story teaches valuable lessons about character development, overcoming challenges, relating to difficult people in your life, fostering courageous faith, and replacing caricatures of God to understand who he really is.

In it, you'll see his challenges and battles, his progress and setbacks, and his transformation from a man controlled by fear into a man of courage and faith.

30 Days with Joshua is written in devotional format. Bite-size chunks of Joshua's life to give you something to chew on daily for a month as God leads you over your faith journey. Rather than slam the book shut, check off "Have Devotions" on your to-do list, and rush on to the next activity, it encourages you to take time to meditate on a single truth every day for 30 days. Time to talk to God, to let him search your heart and show you what's there, and time to formulate a plan to follow Joshua's example for your own journey Home.

If you need insights and encouragement for your

spiritual journey, you'll find it on the pages of *30 Days with Joshua*.

Jump in. An exciting adventure awaits!

"Another fantastic collection of devotions from Steve. The length of these are perfect for reading quick in the morning or anytime you have a few minutes, but they contain some serious food-for-thought that you can think on throughout your day. I love this collection that focuses on Joshua and learning to continue on despite our fear." [Review by Mike]

"I gained insight into the life of Joshua through the pages of this book! Steve's books always make me dig deeper into The Word. Another great book!!!" [Reviewed by Randy]

Available on Amazon.
www.amazon.com/dp/B09B2SSSNC

30 Days with Joseph: Inspiration from Joseph's Spiritual Journey for Yours (A Devotional)

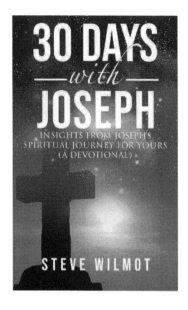

How did Joseph do it?

For 13 years the circumstances of his life went from bad to worse. Slavery. Alleged rapist. Prison convict. He did nothing to deserve such rough treatment.

Yet Joseph never whined or complained. He didn't get angry or depressed. In fact, when he had the chance to exact revenge, he offered mercy, grace, and generosity instead.

How did he do it?

You'll find answers in *30 Days with Joseph,* the second in a series of devotionals that focuses on a Bible character. Each day of the month, you'll accompany Joseph on his spiritual journey and learn how he overcame the challenges he encountered along the way.

And show you how you can too!

"Steve Wilmot's new book, 30 Days with Joseph is a book that you must have!!! Learn about this man of God through the words that Steve writes. These short daily excerpts will have you digging deeper into The Word of

God. Thanks, Steve for sharing your insight about Joseph." [Review by Randy]

"This devotional is a blessing and a great way to deepen your spiritual walk with God. I cannot wait to give as gifts and bless others. Thank you, Steve Wilmot, another great book!" [Review by Connie]

Available on Amazon.
www.amazon.com/dp/B09MVDSPSM

FAQ New Believers Want to Know (And Every Believer Needs to Know)

Would you hand the keys to the family car to your 10-year-old daughter?

Stupid proposition, huh? And yet that's essentially what we do with new believers. We welcome them into the Family of God, then leave them to figure out their next steps alone.

No wonder so many who put their faith in Jesus don't stick around very long. Their decision to follow Jesus was sincere and from the heart, but no one helped them grow a relationship with him. They were left to navigate their spiritual journey on their own.

FAQ New Believers Want to Know (*And Every Believer Needs to Know*) provides a valuable tool to correct this egregious oversight. It provides easy-to-grasp answers that introduce new believers to the basics they need so they can mature in their faith. More mature believers will find it useful to refresh their knowledge and fill in blanks they missed in the early years of their spiritual journey.

FAQ New Believers Want to Know is perfect for small groups and one-on-one mentoring relationships, as well as for personal study.

"We were talking with Bill this spring regarding small groups. He showed us a book that we could consider using for our newly formed small group: Frequently Asked Questions for New Believers. We took the book home and began to read it. At our first small group meeting for the summer, we tackled one of the questions in the book. We had sent out by email the question and supporting scripture in advance, so the group would have opportunity to think about it. The discussion went well and we chose another question for the next meeting, again sending it to the group so that they could prepare.

In the meantime, we had ordered our own book and one of the others in the group ordered their book, too. We continued studying a different question each week, and now all the members have ordered their own books.

These questions have been very helpful in confirming truths for us older believers and younger believers as well. We are thankful for this book and the author."
[Review by Craig]

Available on Amazon.
www.amazon.com/dp/B09WZ96R32

Connect with Steve!

Again, thank you for reading my book of devotionals from Elijah's spiritual journey. If you'd like to connect with me and/or share this book with others, here are a few easy-to-do ideas.

- Swing by and check out my blog. You can find it at my Author Website:
  www.stevewilmotauthor.com.
  You'll find encouraging thoughts and Bible verses to help you on your spiritual journey. Leave a comment. Tell me your story and how you found my books helpful for your pilgrimage toward Home. You can also keep up on other books I'm writing and freebie offers.

- I imagine many of you have blogs, Facebook pages and Twitter accounts and other forms of social media. I'd be grateful if you'd post a review of my book along with a link to www.stevewilmotauthor.com. I'd love it if you left a review at www.Amazon.com, too. A simple recommendation from you could be the gentle push someone needs to pick up this book and benefit from Elijah's experiences as you have.

- Buy a few copies to give away. Share them as birthday or Christmas presents. Use them in a small group study. Be creative. Pass them out to friends. Hand one to your server in a restaurant. (Don't let it replace a nice tip, though!) Place a few copies on a table at your church — but get permission first.

- If you'd like me to speak at your church, organization, or conference, send me an email at doggdad@hotmail.com and I'll see what we can arrange

Made in the USA
Middletown, DE
06 November 2022